ANSWERS FOR YOUR *Marriage*

Bruce and Carol Britten

How your marriage can have true love, friendship, and better sex. What you can do if your husband/wife is selfish, wastes money, has sex outside marriage . . . .

This book is for adults. The right time for young people to read it is: A week before their wedding. Not sooner.
During their youth,
all young people should read our other book,
"Love & Marriage: Questions Young People Ask**"**

OASIS INTERNATIONAL LTD

Answers for Your Marriage
Fourth Edition
Copyright © 2010 by Carol Britten
All rights reserved.

ISBN: 978-1-59452-078-5
ISBN: 1-59452-078-X

Cover and interior design: Robyn Martins

Oasis International is a ministry devoted to fostering a robust and sustainable pan-African publishing industry. For more information, go to oasisint.net.

Why we wrote this book

While we were teaching school in various parts of the world, we wrote two books for young people:

- *Love & Marriage: Questions Young People Ask*
- *Sweet Baby [See page 192.]*

How amazed we felt when those books were printed in countries worldwide.*

Soon we began receiving hundreds of letters—not only from young people, but also from adults. Many of the adults had marriage problems and serious questions about love, sex, child-raising…. Finally we realised, *"We must write a book for adults."*

That's why we wrote: *Answers for your Marriage.* In this book we answer all questions, including those about sex-problems in marriage. Therefore, this book is not for single people who plan to marry someday. It is for adults who are *already married.* Do not leave this book in places where young people may find it.

Readers of this book say:

"My marriage was horrible. I just wanted divorce.
Then I bought *Answers for your Marriage.*
Indeed, there I found answers!"

"My wife and I read this book together.
Each and every chapter brought a
miracle to our marriage!"

"My friends gave me incorrect information about marriage and sex. Now I know the truth!"

---

* China, Colombia, Côte d'Ivoire, Ethiopia, Ghana, India, Kenya, Malawi, Nigeria, Portugal, Slovakia, Sudan, Swaziland, Tanzania, Zimbabwe.

Contents

Letters from people with problems

Chapter 1

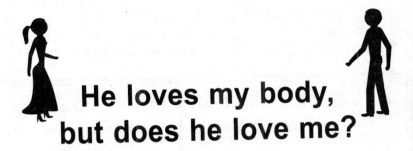

He loves my body, but does he love me?

Dear Bruce and Carol,

My husband loves sex. I give it to him often, but I don't enjoy it. Why? Because I feel he doesn't love me.

Each afternoon when we arrive home from work, I want to talk with him. I want to tell him all about my day, and I want to hear about his. But he asks me no questions and shows no interest in what I've been doing or how I'm feeling. Instead of talking with me, he tells me: "Bring me tea!" and "Make that kid be quiet!"

Then when we get into bed, he wants me to feel sexy. I give him sex, but my heart is not in it—because I know he doesn't care about me. He just enjoys using my body to satisfy himself.

He finishes in only two minutes. Then he immediately falls asleep. And I feel like crying because I realise: *My husband thinks I'm a body with no person inside.*

Often I ask myself, "Why does he hide his thoughts from me? Why doesn't he ever ask about my thoughts and feelings? Does he love me?"

Yours faithfully,
Sarah

Can Sarah and her husband ever have a great marriage? Yes!

The first thing they need is: ***Communication/love.*** 'Communication' means talking with each other freely. 'Love' means unselfish care for the other.

The second thing they need is: Advice on ***Sex.***

This book explains both ***Communication/love*** and ***Sex.***

1) *Communication/love*	2) *Sex*
Your marriage will become more romantic as you choose to *communicate* with each other, and *love* each other unselfishly. In chapters 1 to 5 we explain *communication/love.*	Husbands often say, "My wife isn't sexy." Wives say, "He doesn't know how to satisfy me." In chapters 6 to 8 we explain all about *sex.*

Since this book explains sex, it is for *married* people. Don't leave this book where young people may find it.

If your marriage has a sex-problem, maybe you want to read chapters 6 to 8 first. But we say: Read 1 to 5 first. Why? Because chapters 1 to 5 build the foundation. To have great sex, you must have the foundation shown in picture 2.

Picture 1

Picture 2

Communication [talking from the heart]

Some people say, "A real man doesn't need to talk with his wife." But the fact is: A man will begin to enjoy marriage more when he realises, "It's good for me to *talk freely* with my wife. As I *communicate* with her, we understand each other; our love grows; and our sex becomes more exciting."

There are three levels of communication. Perhaps right now your communication is zero. Don't worry. You and your husband/wife can step up to Level 1 and then to Levels 2 and 3.

When you succeed in reaching Level 3, you will find the joy of romantic friendship and exciting sex.

Level 1: Talk about what happened. Each afternoon when you and your husband/wife arrive home, tell each other what happened during the day. Tell about the car accident you saw, or how your cousin passed his exam ... or whatever happened.

It's amazing that many couples fail to communicate

even at that simple level. They stay in the same house, but they seldom talk.

Don't be like that. Communicate. Every day greet one another with a hug, and talk about what happened during the day. This will become a habit that you both enjoy.

In addition to telling about your day, ask your partner, "What happened in your life today?" That question is important. If a husband never asks his wife about her day, she wonders, "Does he love me?"

We all like to be asked questions that show sincere interest. When anyone asks me questions about my work or my ideas, I think, "Isn't he friendly!"

In marriage, too, we should use questions to show our interest in each other.

Your marriage will improve as you simply talk about your day and ask each other questions. That's Level 1.

But don't stop there. Move on to Level 2.

Level 2: Talk about us. Level 2 of communication is talking about *us:* our money, our children, our relatives, our plans for the future.... For example, a husband can discuss with his wife questions such as: What school should our children attend? Should we ask my cousin to stay with us? Should we buy a new car?

One day Abner and Lydia were discussing his mother. As they talked, they began to disagree and quarrel.

In that case, what should they do? They should continue talking until they reach agreement. But Abner and Lydia didn't do that. Instead, they stopped talking before reaching an agreement. After that they thought, "To avoid another quarrel, we must not talk about 'his mother.'"

Later they had a quarrel about 'money.' Again they stopped talking before reaching an agreement. So, they began avoiding the topic of money.

After some years they had many topics that they couldn't talk about. That killed their communication.

Let's not allow quarrels to kill our communication. Instead, let's discuss each subject in a kind way…and if we begin to disagree, let's continue talking until we agree on a decision.

Level 3: Talk about our feelings. In Level 3 we open the door of our heart, allowing our marriage partner to see our feelings.

Stephen told his wife, "Today my brother got angry and shouted at me. And my father supported him." (That report of *what happened* was Level 1.)

Then Stephen and his wife discussed how this problem could be solved. (That was Level 2 because it involved *us* and *our* relatives.)

After that his wife asked, "How do you *feel* now?"

Stephen replied, "I worry. I fear that our family relationships will decline. I also feel hurt because . . . ." (That sharing of *feelings* was Level 3 communication.)

When we communicate at Level 3,
our joys are doubled because the happiness of one
becomes the happiness of the other.
And our burdens are cut in half
since we share the load.

Not good for a man to be alone

Whenever Joe has a problem, he says to himself, "I won't tell my wife how discouraged I feel today. I'm a *man*. She must not think that I can't handle my problems."

Joe needs to realise:

It's not good for a man to be alone. (Gen. 2[18])
A man and wife are no longer two. They are one.
(Matt. 19[6])

Barriers to communication

In Europe, Asia, Africa, America... many couples fail to communicate. Why? Because they allow barriers to stop their communication . . . barriers such as 'Fear,' 'Too Busy,' and so on.

Fear

It's a sad fact that some husbands make their wives fear them. [See page 150.]   Fear destroys communication. A wife should 'submit' to her husband, but not 'fear' him.

> Wives, submit to your husbands. (Eph. 5 22)
> Husbands love your wives. (Eph. 5 25)
> There is no fear in love. Love removes fear.
> (1 John 4 18)

Too Busy

Dan says, "My wife and I are so busy with our jobs and with church, we have no *time* to communicate."

We reply: Take time to communicate, no matter what. Don't be overly busy. Eliminate some of your activities. And find ways to serve God *together*.

Carol and I find that we communicate extra well after we have done hard work *together*, such as witnessing home-to-home.

Not Listening

Failing to listen is a terrible barrier to communication. Sometimes when Carol is speaking, I think of something I want to say. As she is talking, I'm waiting for a chance to tell her my great idea. But while I'm waiting, I'm *not listening*.

Or sometimes when she is talking, I see that she is mistaken about a small point. While she is still speaking, I'm planning the words I will use to correct her.

But while I'm planning, I'm not listening.

Whenever Carol is speaking, I should focus my mind on her. I should *listen*. Then, if I'm still not sure what she means, I should ask, "Are you saying... or do you mean...?"

> **Each time your husband/wife communicates with you, listen carefully. Not-listening kills communication.**

Father-role and Mother-role

In their first year of marriage, Luke and Priscilla communicated well. Both of them had the feeling, "What joy... to speak with each other *freely about everything!"*

Then their children were born. Soon Priscilla was busy caring for the kids. Luke was busy earning money for them. And they neglected their communication with each other. Their friendship cooled. Now their marriage is nothing more than sharing a house and raising kids.

That kind of marriage is *boring*. To make marriage *romantic*, the husband must not become so busy earning money that he fails to communicate with his wife. And the wife must not get so busy as a mother that she neglects communication with her husband.

Let's never allow anything to reduce our communication.

Hurt

While waiting for the bus, Ruth remembered, "Abel scolded me this morning."

She felt hurt. The hurt was small. Abel had not shouted;

yet his voice seemed cold and unloving.

As she continued thinking about it, the hurt grew. She remembered other times when he had hurt her.

Finally she asked herself, "What can I do about this hurt? If I try to hide it, my communication with Abel this evening will be half-hearted. Under the surface I will still feel hurt. Perhaps I should wait for Abel to say, 'sorry.' No, that won't work because he may not realise how he hurt me. There is only one answer: I must talk with him about the hurt. I will speak honestly, and also respectfully."

That evening when she and Abel were alone, Ruth said softly, "Dear, I think I should let you know that your words this morning hurt me. I've felt hurt all day. Now I feel ashamed for letting such a small thing bother me all day."

After Abel apologized, they were able to communicate and enjoy their evening together.

If Ruth had tried to hide the hurt, what kind of evening (and bed-time) would they have had?

> Ruth's hurt was small. If your marriage has huge hurts, (e.g. adultery or beating) see pages 81-85 and 150-151.

Our reply to Sarah's letter [See page 7.]

> Dear Sarah,
>
> Find a time when you can sit down with your husband and talk with him about your need for better communication. Be respectful. Say something like:
>
> > "Darling, I feel lonely. I feel like you and I are strangers to each other. I'm not saying it's your fault. I think both of us need to make the effort to build our communication."

Choose the right time to say that to your husband. Don't say it when he is tired or hungry. Wait until he is relaxed, and in a quiet place where the two of you can be alone and discuss freely.

Will that discussion change your husband into a good communicator? Hopefully it will help. But perhaps he will still not communicate very well.

Remember this: You must love your husband *even if he doesn't communicate well.* (Also remember: You are not perfect, and your husband has the job of loving you along with your weaknesses.)

After a few weeks, maybe you will tell us, "My husband has improved, but I still need *more* communication." Our reply will be: Don't expect your husband to satisfy your *total* need for communication. Find female friends with whom you can communicate. For example, if one of your relatives dies, you should do two things.

1) Tell your husband how you feel. He may satisfy *part* of your need for communication.

2) Go to some of your female friends and communicate your feelings to them.

Then your need for communication will be met partly by your husband and partly by your female friends.

But notice we said 'female.' If you found a *male* who was good at communicating, you might be tempted to do adultery.

In short, Sarah, do this:

   a) *Have an honest talk with your husband. Let him know that you need communication.*

   b) *Continue to love and respect your husband, even when he is not a good communicator.*

   c) *Don't expect him to satisfy all of your communication needs. Have some female friends.*

Now that you have finished reading this chapter, ask your husband/wife to read it with you. Sit together as one of you reads it aloud. Discuss: "Is our communication at level 1, 2 or 3? How can we reach the next level? What barriers hinder our communication? How can we remove those barriers?"

As you take time/effort to build your communication, your marriage will come alive with romance and sexual joy.

Let me hear your voice. Your voice is sweet.
(Song of Songs 2 14)

My sweetheart, my bride! Your love delights me. (4 10)

He is my *lover*, and he is my *friend*. (5 16)

I belong to him, and he desires me. (7 10)

Chapter **2**

 **Our love is lost**

Dear Bruce and Carol,

In our first year of marriage, my wife and I loved each other passionately. But now our lovely feelings have disappeared. Our marriage has turned ice-cold. We don't talk much. It's hard for us to say, "I love you." And our sex is going down-hill.

Neither of us has fallen in love with anyone else. But we have stopped feeling love for each other.

I doubt that our marriage will ever be happy.

Our love is lost.

Please help us,

Joel

When we answered Joel's letter, Carol and I were glad to tell him how his marriage can become romantic.

Joel's problem is: *He doesn't know what love is.*

In fact, most people are ignorant about love. All over Europe, Africa, America, and Asia; people talk about love, but they don't understand it.

What is love?

Love is choosing to do kind, unselfish deeds for the other. Love is giving and forgiving. Love is helping and thanking.

Love is not just a *feeling*. Love is what we <u>do</u>.

Doesn't everyone know that? No! Many people think, "Love can get lost."

The truth is: *Love cannot get lost.*

A key can get lost. When I lose a key, I cannot find it no matter how I try. But I cannot lose love. Why? Because *love is action. I choose my actions.*

If I choose to be kind and helpful, I'm choosing to love.

If I choose to be unkind, I'm choosing not to love.

If I choose to be unkind, I must not say "My love is lost."

If I do not love my wife, it's my fault. I'm responsible to love her.

My *duty* is: Choose to love my wife with kind actions.

The feeling of love

Listen to this: The *'feeling of love'* is not the same as *'love.'* What is the 'feeling of love'? It's the exciting feeling of, "She loves me, and I love her." Millions of songs are written about this marvelous feeling.

Yet few people understand that even in a good marriage, the feeling of love rises...falls...rises...falls....

Today a husband may have a strong feeling of love for his wife, but tomorrow that feeling may fall...the next day it may rise...but soon after that it may fall again. Why? Because the feeling of love is just a *feeling.* Our feelings always change.

We humans have many different feelings. Sometimes we feel angry, sometimes lonely, and sometimes we feel in love. We don't have the same feeling every day.

Have you ever felt happy every day for a month? No, happiness is a feeling and so it comes and goes. All feelings rise, fall, rise.... But *love* can remain the same.

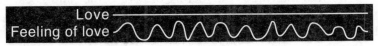

After the wedding

On their wedding day, the bride and groom promise to love each other until death. Does that mean they are promising to have a *feeling* every day? No. When they promise to 'love,' they are promising to **do** kind actions.

Will they have a 'feeling of love'? Yes, but not every day. Some days they may feel tired or troubled. They may feel no love. And that's okay. God never says, "Try to *feel*." He says, "Love." He says, "Love is kind."

So, every day a husband and wife should choose to do kind things for each other. Their feelings will rise and fall, but they shouldn't worry about that. Their job is: "Love each other with kind words/deeds, and continue doing that daily, no matter if your feelings go down or up." (1 Corinth. 13 [4])

Sometimes I feel like serving my wife; other times my feelings beg me to be selfish. *Love* means: I decide to care for my wife. I comfort and encourage her, no matter if my feelings tell me, "Be selfish."

Of course, I'm human. Sometimes I fail to be kind. But I must never say, "My love is lost." I can love her if I choose to. Love is not outside my control.

Is there hope for Joel's marriage?

Joel says, "My love is lost."

God says, "Love your wife. Each day choose to care for her."

What about the 'feeling of love'? Can Joel's marriage ever have that nice, romantic feeling? Yes!

In normal marriages the feeling of love comes and goes, but in Joel's marriage the feeling is *gone*. He no longer has any days when he feels love for her.

But that can change.

Here's a command and a promise that can change Joel's marriage . . . and yours!

The Command

**Even if you have no feeling of love, choose to love your husband/wife. How?
Be extra careful to be helpful, generous, polite, patient, forgiving . . . .**

That's a difficult command. But here's a wonderful promise.

The Promise

As you do those kind actions, soon your feeling of love will return!

You don't need to go year after year with no feeling of love. That exciting feeling can return. It will return as you choose to be kind.

Of course, the feeling of love is just a feeling. It will rise and fall. *But if you continue doing kind actions, the feeling of love will never stay down for long.*

Your love delights me.
(Song 4^{10})

In the first week of her marriage, Eunice felt so happy to be married to Philip.

But in the second week she discovered, "Philip is not always sweet."

Her feelings for him began to cool.

Yet, she remembered the words she said on her wedding day, "I promise to love this man . . . ."

Slowly she realised, *"I promised.* Now I must love him even when he is disagreeable . . . and I hope he will love me, even when I'm difficult to live with."

So she decided, "I will <u>do</u> something for him. I'll cook a *nice* meal!" As she was cooking, her feelings changed. She began feeling love for him again. Her <u>action</u> of love (cooking that meal) helped to bring back her <u>feeling</u> of love.

> Doing unselfish deeds brings back the feeling of love.

Don't be a slave to your feelings

Caleb loved his wife; but the secretary at work wore short, tight skirts. Soon Caleb realised, *"She smiles at me...she wants me!"*

His feelings for his wife began to cool. His new feelings told him, "Undress the secretary, try her young body."

Can he escape that trap? Yes! He can decide, "I will do nothing to that secretary, and I will be extra kind to my wife."

As he does that, his feelings for his wife will grow; and his feelings for the secretary will cool. Then he will avoid the sorrow that adultery brings to a home. [Adultery: pages 81-85 and 148.]

I chose to tell my eyes not to look lustfully at a girl. (Job 31[1])

Facts about 'Love' and the 'Feeling of love.'

Fact 1
Love is action. It is doing whatever is kind and unselfish. You can choose to love.

Fact 2
The *feeling of love* is just a feeling. Even in a good marriage, the feeling rises and falls.

Fact 3
If you stop doing kind actions, your feeling of love will disappear totally.

Fact 4
If your feeling of love has disappeared, bring it back. How? Be careful to do kind, unselfish actions.

In his letter [page 17] Joel said, "My wife and I no longer feel love."

Here's our reply:

Dear Joel,

On your wedding day you promised to love your wife until death. That was a promise to God. Keep that promise. (Ecc. 5⁴) How? Decide, "I will love my wife by giving myself daily to do helpful, kind things for her."

As you do that, soon you will notice, "I'm starting to have that feeling again—the nice feeling that makes me sing, *'I love her!'*"

Of course, that feeling will rise and fall.

Your job is: Love your wife every day, no matter whether the feeling happens to be high or low that day.

Then as years pass, the loving feeling in your marriage will grow stronger. Feelings always have ups and downs, but the ups will grow more exciting, and the downs will become less frequent. So your marriage will grow more romantic.

Chapter 3

Continue in love

When a girl is near the guy she hopes to marry, she is careful to avoid any anger or impatience. And if he is interested in her, he is careful to be polite and generous.

Then they marry. And what happens after that?

They relax.

She thinks, "Now I'm married. I no longer fear that I will fail to get a husband. I can relax. I can stop being so careful to be kind and respectful."

Her husband is the same way. After the wedding he tells himself, "Now she's my *woman*." He no longer tries to think of her needs. Instead, he relaxes and thinks of himself. When he feels hurt because of something she did, he doesn't forgive her. He allows himself to say hurtful words to her.

She does the same to him. So the hurts grow larger.

I promise to love....

WEDDING

Now she's my wife. I can stop trying so hard to be kind. I can relax.

I'm married. Now I can relax. I can stop being careful to respect him.

WRONG ATTITUDES AFTER THE WEDDING

Their marriage could improve if one of them would decide, "I will make the effort to be kind, even when my husband/wife is not kind to me." But that is hard work. So they don't do it. They are relaxing.

Soon their *feeling of love* disappears, and each of them begins thinking, "Can our marriage ever be romantic?"

God says, "Yes. Decide to love each other."

That means: Decide to be patient, generous, polite and respectful. Continue doing that year after year. Don't relax.

Young people are surprised when we tell them, "After your wedding, don't relax. Instead of relaxing, be *careful* to continue giving kind words and deeds...every day. That's not easy. It requires effort. You must *work* at it."

They ask, "If I must *work* at loving my partner, doesn't that make marriage cold and unexciting?"

We reply, "No! Work at loving your wife with kind deeds. Work at loving your husband with respect. Yes, *work* at it. Do it even when your selfish nature tells you, 'Relax.' *Then your marriage will never grow cold, but will actually grow more and more romantic.*"

God says to husbands

Love your wife as you love yourself. (Eph. 5 [33])

'Love' means: Be polite and self-giving. Do not demand you own way. Do not be quick to get angry. Forgive. (1 Corinth. 13 [5])

Be unselfish. Think of your wife's needs. She is physically weaker. Treat her as your partner. If you treat her right, your prayers will have more power. (1 Peter 3 [7])

God says to Wives

Submit to your husband. That is God's plan.
(Col. 3 [18] and Eph. 5 [22-24])

Be careful to respect your husband. If he doesn't believe the Bible, your love and your conduct will help him to believe. You won't need to preach at him or say a word. (1 Pet. 3 [1])

You older women must train young women to love their husbands. (Titus 2 [4])

Chapter 4

Our own marriage

Bruce: When I was a young man, a girl named Carol joined our church. Everyone liked her. She was cheerful, and she loved Christ so much.

Carol: We young people often witnessed at the college. And on Fridays we gathered children into a home for 'Bible Story Hour.'

Our Youth-Leader was a young man named Bruce. I told myself, "All children love Bruce. He will be a good father, and a good husband for some fortunate girl."

Later I was so excited when he asked *me* to marry him.

Then we moved from America to Swaziland where Bruce began teaching science. Our daughter and son were born, but our marriage became unhappy.

Bruce: I was busy preaching everywhere, but at home I wasn't careful to be a friend to my wife.

Carol: I felt unloved. Therefore, some days I refused to speak to Bruce. Then one day a lady at church said, "I used to go for days without speaking to my husband, but God gave me power to change."

That day I promised God, "Instead of keeping silent, I will talk with Bruce about how I feel."

Bruce: Carol told me how hurt and unloved she felt. I realised: I must change. Eph 5$^{25-31}$ showed me how to be a better husband.

Carol: It was a miracle how our marriage improved! Then one day Bruce told me, "It's good that we pray with the kids, but we also need to pray together—just you and me."

Now each day we pray for one country of the world... then we pray for friends...then for each other. (I love listening as my husband prays for me.)

When our daughter was 16 she told us, "If I marry, I want a relationship with my husband like you two have."

Bruce: Our marriage-love is a *blessing,* especially in times of trouble. Recently we had *big* trouble. I was in the hospital very sick. There a lady doctor told me, "Bruce, I'm sorry. You are HIV+."

"Are you sure?" I asked in surprise.

"Yes. We've tested your blood twice."

"But I've never had sex with anyone except my wife."

"Maybe you got HIV from a blood transfusion," she said.

"Doctor," I said, "please listen. When I die, I know I'll go to heaven—just because Christ died for my sins. Doctor, if you accept Christ...."

She listened, but she didn't choose to accept Christ.

Carol: I was shocked that Bruce was HIV+. Yet I was sure that he never had sex with anyone but me. We both knew that our Creator demands: *Sex is for marriage only.* We obeyed that law.

Bruce: One day a friend told me, "Some people are saying, 'Bruce likes to preach against adultery, but now his HIV shows his own sin.'"

Still, I was glad to know: Carol trusts me.

Carol: The doctor tested *my* blood. Later she told me, "You have no HIV. But we tested Bruce's blood again. He is definitely HIV+."

Bruce: I told Carol, "People with AIDS get sores in their mouths. Look, now I have those sores. Let's continue asking God for healing, and let's also remember: God is good, even if he chooses not to heal me."

Carol: I asked friends to pray. With tears I phoned our children. We promised to pray, and to believe together that God has the best plan, even if he did not heal Bruce.

Bruce: Then came the day I'll never forget. The same lady doctor told me, "Bruce, you are __*not*__ HIV+. Now your blood-tests show __*no*__ HIV."

"It's a miracle!" I exclaimed.

"I don't believe in miracles," she replied. "The previous tests must have been an error."

I phoned Carol. How we praised God! And I realised: Even the sores in my mouth are suddenly gone!

Carol: With tears of joy I told everyone the great news!

Bruce: I don't say, "God healed me because I have more faith than other Christians." Elisha had great faith, but God chose not to heal him. He died of disease. (2 Kings 13 [14])

And many Christians who take the gospel to far countries die of diseases such as malaria.

If God had decided not to heal me, we would still love and serve him.

When I got out of hospital, a neighbour lady told me, "Bruce, many people claim to love Jesus, but your wife *really* loves him. Whenever she talked about your HIV, I could see that *she was going to keep on loving Jesus— whether he healed you or took you to heaven.*"

How I became a Christian

Carol: When I was age 15, my elder sister surprised me by saying, "Carol, please become a Christian."

How could she say that? I've *always* been a Christian (I thought). I attend church. I've been baptised. I never do big sins. *I am a Christian.* How can she say, "Please *become* a Christian? Who does she think she is? I'm as good as she!"

Still, she took me with her to youth camp. There I heard a preacher say, "Everyone has sinned. You are sinful!"

That surprised me! In my eyes I was a baptised good-girl.

But in God's eyes I was a *sinner!* I didn't want to believe it, yet I heard him read it straight from the Bible:

> No one is good. All have sinned. (Rom. 3 [12 and 23])

At that camp I also heard that Jesus came to earth and suffered for the sins I've done. That's why God can forgive me.

> God so loved the world that he gave his only Son,
>   so that whoever believes in him
> will not go to hell, but to heaven. (John 3 [16])

Then I realised: No one can do enough good to earn heaven. Instead of thinking that my good works can take me to heaven, I must confess my sins and believe that Jesus died in my place. I must stop trusting my good works. I must begin to trust Jesus!

That day I prayed, asking Jesus to save me from hell.

My prayer to become a Christian

Lord Jesus, I'm sinful. I deserve hell. But the Bible says: You suffered in my place. Today I trust you to forgive my sins. Now I know that I will go to heaven. Why? Because *you* died for me—not because of any good work I've done.

Now I will work for you just because I love you.

My sister was so excited when I told her, "I've become a Christian!"

Bruce: We hope you will ask Jesus to be your Lord and your Saviour. (Rom. 10 [9])

Then let's take the Good News to our neighbours, and to all nations.

The Holy Spirit will give you power to witness in your home area and to all nations. (Acts 1 [8], Mat. 28 [18-20])

Chapter **5**

Improve your marriage

On the day you become a Christian, the Holy Spirit begins to give you power. With his power you can improve your marriage. How? Do these three romance-building actions:

1) Give appreciation.   2) Do kind actions.   3) Complain less.

1) Give appreciation

Every husband/wife needs to hear, "I appreciate the way you work hard to care for our kids. Thanks for helping my mother. And I appreciate the way you . . . ."

If we receive no appreciation, we feel hurt.

While Caleb and Rachel were visiting his relatives, she asked him, "Please drive me to the shop. I didn't bring enough nappies for the baby."

"Why can't you plan ahead?" Caleb snapped.

He said that in front of his relatives . . . the very people Rachel hoped to impress.

How loved she would have felt if Caleb had thanked her (in front of his relatives) for one of her good points!

Another man told us, "I get no thanks from my wife, even though I never chase girls." His wife replied, "Each day when he arrives home, he just says, *'Bring dinner.'* I wish he'd say, 'You cook well, and you look nice.'"

Listen everyone: In private and in public, look for opportunities to praise your partner. Give appreciation, no matter how little you receive. (Prov. 12 ^{25})

People ask, "Instead of *trying* to say appreciative words, shouldn't I wait until I naturally feel like saying them?"

Answer: No, don't wait. Give appreciation, even when you don't feel like it. We must *work* at giving appreciation. We must not relax.

Your selfish nature says, "You receive *little* appreciation; so give *little*."

Don't allow your selfish nature to rule. Give appreciation.

How to begin. One man decided, "I will give my wife appreciation." Then he wrote this chart:

Things I like about my wife	How I will show my appreciation
1) She is a good mother to our children.	1) Often I will tell the children, "You kids are fortunate to have a wonderful mother."
2) She welcomes guests into our home.	2) I will tell her, "I appreciate the way you treat visitors."
3) Sometimes she does kind things for my parents.	3) I will compliment her each time she does something for them.
4) She teaches Sunday School faithfully.	4) I'll buy a gift and write on it, "Thanks for serving God."
5) People like the way she is joyful and talkative.	5) I will tell her how my sister told me, "Your wife is pleasant and friendly."

Make a chart like that for your husband/wife. How? Do this:

   a) Ask yourself, "What do I honestly like about my partner?" Write five things. [Even if there are many things you don't like about him/her, you can certainly find five good qualities.]

   b) Write how you plan to show him/her that you appreciate those five qualities.

He will get better. If you show appreciation to your partner, he/she will *improve!*

For example, if your husband shows some interest in the children, and you tell him how much you appreciate that—he will improve and show *more* interest in them.

Criticism will never help him to improve. Appreciation will!

A reporter asked a thousand teachers, "How could your headmaster make you try harder to be a better teacher?"

Most teachers replied, "I would try harder if he would *begin to appreciate my efforts.*"

Yes, begin today to give appreciation to your husband/wife. You will be surprised how your marriage will improve. Also give appreciation to your kids. They will improve!

> **Appreciation** will help him/her **to improve.**

2) Do kind actions

The second way you can improve your marriage is: Do kind things. Here are examples:

Husband

● Tell your wife, "I love you," and then tell her one reason why you love her. Her face will brighten as you mention something about her that you love.

● Take time to sit and talk with her. Let her know your thoughts and feelings.

● Bring her a gift and say, "This gift is just because I love you." (Never say, "You must 'pay' for it by giving me special favours in bed.")

● Be careful how you speak to her when you are angry.

❃ Help her with the work at home. When your children
see how nicely you treat her, they will think, "We feel
safe because Dad loves Mum."

❃ Look for her good qualities. Tell her often how glad you
are for those qualities.

❃ Tell her parents how you appreciate their daughter.

❃ When she does something kind, thank her! The two most
loving words are, "Thank you."

❃ Every day pray in two ways:
a) with your wife and children.
b) with just your wife—the two of you together.

Wife

❃ When your husband comes home from work, greet him with
a hug and cheerful words. Don't have a sour face. Show that
you are happy to see him.

❃ Tell the children how much you appreciate 'Daddy.'
Josiah came home from work feeling dead tired. Then his
little daughter told him, "Mum says you work hard to take
care of us." Suddenly he forgot his tiredness!

❃ Look for his good qualities. Mention them often.

❃ If someone says nice things about your husband, tell him.
Don't think, "If I tell him, he will get proud."

❃ Always wear clothes that don't tempt men. But sometimes
at night get into bed before your husband, and let him find
you naked under the sheet . . . ready for love. He will feel,
"My wife doesn't show her body to other men—only to me.
She loves me!"

Perhaps you are thinking, "Those ideas don't fit my culture." Okay. Think of your own ideas. Each day ask yourself, "What kind actions can I do for my wife/husband today?"

Kindness takes effort. It takes effort to think of ideas. It takes effort to do them. Yes, love is work. But do it! As you take time to do kind actions, amazing joy will enter your marriage.

3) Complain less

John says, "My wife always complains, *'This house is small... our car is old... I never have money to do my hair....'* She just goes on and on—as if nothing's right."

Anna says, "Every time my husband enters the house, he complains, *'Must you cook the meat that way? Why are your clothes lying on my chair...?'*"

A good way to improve your marriage is: *Complain less.* Yes, next time you are tempted to complain, stop and ask yourself, "Do I really need to complain about this? Instead of complaining, is there a better way? Perhaps I can wait for a day when the meat is cooked right and then say, 'This is great... please cook it like this often.' And I can easily move her clothes from my chair (without complaining). Many things are too small to complain about."

I will say, "Thank you," more often. I will complain less.

Love covers (pays no attention to) many failures.
(1 Peter 4 [8])

If you always criticize each other, watch out,
you will destroy your loving friendship. (Gal. 5 [15])

Give love, even if you don't receive it.

Some people ask, "Why should I,

       1) show appreciation,
       2) do kind actions,
       3) and complain less?

"My partner doesn't love me in those ways. Why should I give love to him/her?"

Jesus has the answer. He says, "Let me fill your cup with love. I will fill it full. Then, instead of *seeking* love, you can *give* it. Yes, enjoy my love, and give love to people." (John 4 10-14)

How beautiful you are,
my darling.
Your eyes are doves.
    (Song of Songs 1 15)

How handsome you are,
my husband.
Our wedding-bed is
beautiful. (Song 1 16)

Chapter 6

Satisfy his/her sex-needs

Some say, "God doesn't want anyone to enjoy sex."
The truth is: *God wants a husband and his wife to find great pleasure in sex.*

In the book of the Bible called 'Song of Songs,' the husband says to his wife:

> How sweet is your love, my darling, my bride!
> The beautiful smell of your love is better than
> the richest spice. (4 [10])
> Your thighs are perfectly curved
> like jewels. (7 [1])

> God wants you
> to enjoy sex
> in your marriage.
> (Prov. 5 [18-20])

And the wife says to her husband:

> Let your lips cover me with kisses. (1 [2])
> My lover lies between my breasts. (1 [13])
> His mouth is sweet.
> He is my lover and my friend.... (5 [16])
> Come, my lover, let's go to the hills...
> There I will give you my love! (7 [11-12])

Yes, God's plan is: *Enjoy* sex in your marriage.

Unfortunately, some husbands don't even try to excite or satisfy their wives. They say, "A good wife should not enjoy sex. She must just relax while I do it to her."

And some wives don't want to enjoy sex. They get into bed with the attitude, "If you must have it, then do it to me. But hurry. I need my sleep."

How different that is from the above verses where the wife says, "Let your lips cover me with kisses.... His mouth is sweet.... He is my lover and my friend.... Come...I will give you my love!" (Song of Songs 1 [2], 5 [16], 7 [12])

Your job is: Satisfy the sex-needs of your wife/husband.

God says to you, "I created your wife/husband with needs. What needs? The need for love and the need for sex. You must satisfy those needs—not only when you feel like it, but also when you don't. You have the responsibility (and the pleasure) of satisfying his/her needs for love and sex. That's your job."

> A husband should satisfy the sexual needs of his wife, and she should satisfy his sexual needs. (1 Corinth. 7 [3])

Listen, husband. Your wife should not go day after day feeling hungry for sex. You must give her what she needs.

Listen, wife. It's not good for your husband to go into town feeling hungry for sex. Satisfy him at home.

Why does God command us to satisfy the sex-needs of our husband/wife? Because God wants us to enjoy love and sexual satisfaction in marriage. God does not want adultery.

Your body belongs to your husband/wife.

Husband, on your wedding day, God gave your body to your wife. Now, when she needs sex, she has a body to satisfy her. Which body? Yours. Your body is now hers.

Wife, your body is no longer yours. It's now his.

> The wife's body belongs to her husband.
> The husband's body belongs to his wife. (1 Corinth. 7 [3])

Some wives think, "Since my husband refuses to buy furniture, I will give him no sex this month."

Please, wife, don't think like that. Your body belongs to your husband. Don't think that you have the right to hold back sex from him.

We asked 100 people, "Does your husband/wife satisfy your sex-needs?"   80 said, "No, he/she does not."

If your husband/wife is not satisfied, do what God tells you: Satisfy him/her. Begin today. Put down this book; go satisfy him/her right now. *Enjoy it!*

When he/she asks for sex, usually you should say 'yes,' but there are 3 times when you may say 'no.'

1) You may say 'no' if the two of you *agree.*

> Do not refuse to satisfy each other. If both of you *agree* not to have sex for a *brief time* so you can pray more, when the brief time is over, continue satisfying each other's sexual needs. Otherwise Satan may tempt you to do adultery.
> (1 Corinth. 7 5)

When a husband wants sex, his wife may say, "I'm tired. Let's not...okay?"

He may reply, "Okay," or he may reply, "Let's do it." If he says, "Let's do it," they should do it.

Similarly, when a wife asks for sex, he may say, "Not today...okay?"

She may reply, "Okay," or she may say, "Let's do it." If she says, "Let's do it," they should do it.

So, who decides—the husband or the wife?

Answer: The one who needs sex is the one who decides.

  * If the husband asks for sex and she prefers not, <u>he</u> decides either, "Let's do it," or "Let's not."
  * If the wife asks for sex and he prefers not, <u>she</u> decides either, "Let's do it," or "Let's not."

2) You may say 'no' if it's for a *brief time.*

> A husband may say, "Let's have sex now."
> She may say, "Please, let's wait a brief time."
> He asks, "How long?"
> She says, "Maybe three weeks?"
> He says, "I prefer now."
> She says, "Tomorrow let's have red-hot sex!"
> He says, *"Okay, tomorrow. Thanks, Honey!"*

They did well. They obeyed the above verse, (1 Corinth. 7 5).
They talked...they *'agreed'* on a *'brief time.'*

3) You may say 'no' if you think you could catch HIV.

If your husband/wife falls into adultery, it is right for you to say, "He/She should be tested for HIV. If he/she is HIV+, we must do whatever the doctor says so that HIV will not pass from her/him to me. It would not be good for both of us to die and leave our children alone." [See pages 111-118.]

One of you may need sex more often than the other.

Sometimes a wife desires sex daily, but her husband prefers it weekly. In other cases, the husband desires it daily and the wife needs it less often.

Do your best to give your husband/wife sex as often as he/she desires it, even if it's every day.

Statistics show: The average husband desires sex 3 times more often than his wife.

Don't say to your husband/wife, "You need sex <u>too</u> often. Something is wrong with you."

Instead, satisfy him/her. Don't refuse. If you refuse, Satan will temp him/her to do adultery. (1 Corinth. 7 3-5)

If I do adultery, is it *my* sin? Answer: Yes, it's *your* sin.

People like to say, "My adultery was not my sin—it was the fault of my husband/wife—because he/she didn't satisfy me."

God says, "If you do adultery, it's your sin." (Ex. 20 14) If your husband/wife does not satisfy you, Satan will tempt you, but Satan cannot force you. You have power to say 'no' to adultery (1 Corinth. 10 13). If you don't say 'no,' it's your sin.

God wants you to enjoy sex — with no fear of HIV.

*If you and your wife were HIV- on your wedding day,
and if you continue having sex with each other only,
you will not get HIV.
You are free to enjoy any kind of sex with each other,
with no fear of HIV.*

Let's teach our children and all young people, "Obey God. Don't have sex before marriage. Then on your wedding day you will be HIV⁻. Marry a person who obeys God and is HIV⁻. Then you can enjoy your husband/wife, with no fear of HIV."

Sex in marriage is beautiful.

How delightful is your love, my bride! Your lips, my bride, are as sweet as honey....
(Song 4 [10-11])

Sex outside marriage is bitterly sinful.

The lips of another lady drip honey, but in the end she is bitter. Do not go near her door. My son, drink from your own well.
(Proverbs 5 [3, 4, 8, 15])

Is it okay for a person to remain single? Yes.

Perhaps your daughter or son will say, *"I just want to serve Jesus. I will never marry."* Is that okay?

Yes, the Bible says it's good to remain single.

The Bible also says it's good to marry.

Why is it good to remain single? Because single people can give themselves fully to serving God. They have no cares of married life to hold them back. (1 Corinth. 7 [1 and 32-34])

Why is it good to marry? Because marriage satisfies our sex-needs. (1 Corinth. 7 [2-9]) Also married people can bear children and serve God together with them. (Joshua 24 [15])

Therefore, each person is free to choose,
either to remain single, or to marry.
Both are good.
*But remember this: Married people **and** single people*
must obey God's laws for sex.

God's laws for sex

1) Married people must have sex with no one except their own husband/wife. (Heb. 13 ^{4})

2) Single people must not have sex with anyone. (1 Thes. 4 $^{3-8}$, 1 Tim. 5 $^{1-2}$, 2 Tim. 2 ^{22}, Deut. 22 $^{13-29}$)

These laws were not made by a church committee. These are the laws of our Creator and Judge.

Each person will be judged by God for the good or bad he did in his body. (2 Corinth. 5 ^{10})

In the following letter, Sam says his wife doubts that a Christian should get *pleasure* from sex.

> *My wife never wants to get excited during sex. She says, "Sex gives us children; that's enough. We Christians shouldn't enjoy sexy pleasures."*
>
> *When I say, "Let's use new positions to make our sex more fun," she replies, "No. Prostitutes do that."*
>
> *Satan whispers to me, "Divorce her and take a wife who enjoys sex."*
>
> *But I always remember: On my wedding-day I promised to be faithful to her until death.*
>
> *In my office at work I see attractive ladies, but I never say or do anything sinful to them. Why? Because Christ will judge all sins. (2 Pet. 3 $^{7-11}$)*
>
> *My wife is a good woman. I love her. I just wish she would allow herself to enjoy our sex. Please write a letter that she and I can read together.*
>
> *Sam*

In our letter to Sam and his wife, we said: Children are a blessing—but children are not the only purpose of sex. God wants you to *enjoy* sex.

As husband and wife, you are 100% free to give each other sexual pleasures . . . in *whatever* ways both of you enjoy.

Enjoy looking at each other's body.
Play together, in the light or in the dark.
Enjoy touching. (Gen. 2 24-25, Song of Songs 2 6, 5 1, 6 3)
God has given you a wonderful job.
That job is: *Satisfy each other.* (1 Corinth. 7 3-5)
What a nice, exciting job that is!

Prostitutes and their customers are *not* the ones who enjoy sex the most.

Who enjoys sex most? Is it people who live in sin? No! It's husbands and wives who love God, and save sex for each other only.

"My bride is a garden filled with delicious fruit.
"The garden is locked to all others."
(Song of Songs 4 12-13)

"Come, my husband, come to your garden. Eat its fruit. (4 16)
"Seal me in your heart, (have sex with me only) because jealousy burns like fire." (8 6)

Chapter 7

Know how to satisfy

Dear Bruce and Carol,

When we are in bed, my husband is too fast. He kisses and fondles me for just a short time. Then, before I have time to get excited, he enters me and ejaculates. Then he goes to sleep. And I feel unsatisfied.

That's why I don't like to have sex often. Now he's complaining that I don't satisfy him often enough.

How can we begin to satisfy each other?

In Christ,

Esther

To satisfy each other you need two things:

    a) 'Communication/love' (See chapters 1-5.)

    b) 'Know how' (See this chapter 7.)

'Communication/love' must come first. That's why the first 5 chapters of this book concentrate on communication and love.

If you have not yet read chapters 1-5, go back and read them now. This chapter on 'Know how' will not help you unless your marriage has 'Communication/love.'

The foundation must come first.

If you have read 1-5, and you are busy improving your 'Communication/love,' this chapter will help you and your husband/wife to succeed in satisfying each other's sex-needs.

In this chapter we will explain sex clearly. Don't forget: This book is for married people. Never leave this book in places where young people may find it. Young people should read it one week before their wedding. Not sooner.

There are four steps in sex: Prepare... Loveplay... Enter... Relax afterwards.

Step One
Prepare

Prepare for sex in the following ways:

a) **Forgive.** Settle your quarrels before bed-time. If the two of you had a quarrel during the day, take time to discuss it, apologize, and forgive one another.

> Do not let the sun go down on your anger. (Eph. 4 26)

When you obey that verse, you get into bed knowing, "We've forgiven one another. Our relationship is close. Now we can enjoy each other."

It's a different story for couples who do not forgive before bed-time. They try to enjoy sex, but the pleasure is spoiled by the bitterness in their hearts.

b) Be neat and clean. Dan says, "At work the secretaries dress smartly, but every afternoon when I arrive home, my wife is dressed like an old woman."

Martha says, "When my husband doesn't wash himself, his body smells. That turns me off."

A husband and wife should be careful to show each other: *I want to be neat and clean when I'm with you.*

c) Lock the door. Put a lock on your bedroom door. A wife cannot enjoy sex if she fears that someone may enter the room at any moment.

d) Undress. God planned that a husband and wife should enjoy being naked together. So they don't need to feel embarrassed. When they are alone in their bedroom, the husband kisses his wife as he slowly removes all her clothes, and she does the same for him. It's a *holy joy* for a husband and wife to undress each other. (Gen. 2 25)

Step Two
Loveplay

Husband, you can help your wife to enjoy sex. How? Spend a long time in loveplay.

'Loveplay' means: Taking time to 'play'…to build each other's excitement…before you enter her.

During loveplay a husband and wife hug and kiss. They also 'fondle' one another by touching and rubbing each other's body.

In her letter on page 42, Esther says, "My husband is too fast. He fondles me for just a short time. Then, before I have time to get excited, he enters me."

Many husbands make that mistake. What mistake? They hurry.

They spend too little time in loveplay.

The husband kisses his wife once, then he immediately enters her...he gets satisfied...he goes to sleep.

Because of his hurry, his wife doesn't get satisfied. And he isn't very happy because he realises, "Somehow I failed to satisfy my wife."

Why didn't she reach the point of feeling satisfied? Because he didn't spend enough time in loveplay before he entered.

It's good to spend time in loveplay. In the Bible we find a husband and wife taking a long time for loveplay:

> She says, "Kiss me. Let my lover come...taste my choice fruits." (Song of Songs 1[2] and 4[16])
>
> He says, "Your thighs are jewels...your mouth is sweet...." (Song 7[1 and 9])

His body and her body

A man and wife need to know some things about one another's body. A man's body is simple. He has only one very sensitive area. That's his penis. When his wife fondles it, he gets excited quickly.

A woman's body is not so simple. In fact, women easily understand a man's body, but many men do not understand a woman's body.

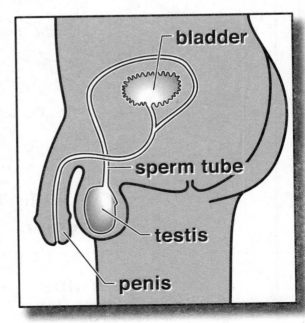

A woman has *two* sensitive areas: her 'vagina' and her 'clitoris.' Her *most* sensitive area is her clitoris.

The clitoris is outside the vagina. In fact, it is about 4 cm from the vagina.

Unfortunately, many husbands think that the only way to build a wife's excitement is to put a finger inside her vagina. The truth is: A woman will become *more* excited if he uses his fingers to fondle the area *outside her vagina* where her inner lips and *clitoris* are.

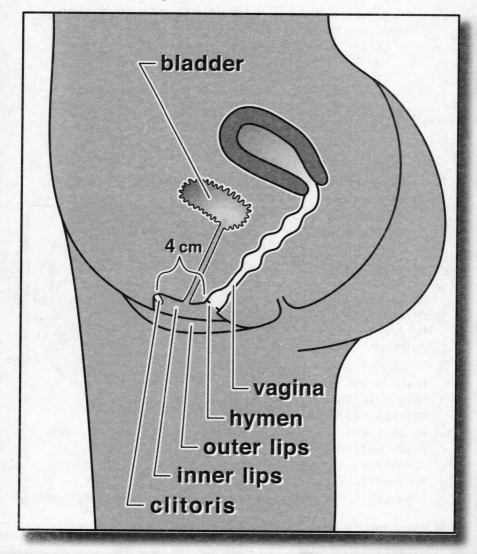

During loveplay a husband should fondle both the vagina and the clitoris, *but especially the clitoris.*

Spend plenty of time — never hurry

A man's body is faster than a woman's. If a wife fondles her husband's penis for just a few *seconds,* he gets excited, his penis gets hard, and he is ready for sex.

A woman becomes excited *slowly.* She needs about *twenty minutes* of loveplay in order to get really excited and ready for sex.

Therefore, a husband should spend many minutes in loveplay, even though his body needs only a few seconds.

Listen husbands: Don't obey your 'natural desires.' A man's natural desires tell him, "Look, your wife is undressing for bed. She's beautiful. Hurry! Lay her on the bed, kiss her quickly, immediately enter her, ejaculate, remove your penis, and go to sleep."

Result: The wife doesn't have time to become very excited, and so she doesn't reach the point of feeling, "Now my sex-need is satisfied."

Therefore, husbands, do this: Before you enter your wife, help her excitement to grow. In other words, *spend much time in loveplay.*

Here are some ideas on how to do loveplay.

Loveplay step A: Upper body

A good way to begin loveplay is: Fondle your wife's upper body. 'Upper body' means above the waist.

Unfortunately, some husbands ignore the upper body... they hurry to fondle her sex organs.

But a husband who is a good lover doesn't hurry. He takes time to hug and kiss his wife's upper body—her mouth, neck, breasts, etc.

Not all women are the same. Some enjoy having their breasts fondled, others don't.

Therefore, ladies, as your husband is loving you, show him where you wish to be fondled. Talk freely...and show him what you like.

During loveplay a husband and wife are <u>free</u> to tell each other what feels good, and what doesn't. Yes, <u>talk</u> during loveplay. Enjoy it!

Loveplay step B: Lower body

After he spends time fondling her upper body, she will move his hand down to her vagina.

He can lie near her, and put his left arm under her head while his right hand fondles her vagina.

As a woman becomes excited, her vagina produces a liquid that helps to lubricate it.

Sometimes a woman may produce much liquid; other times her vagina may remain dry. If it's dry, the husband should lubricate his fingers with 'water soluble lubricating jelly' (buy from a Chemist), or with 'body lotion.' (If you choose 'body lotion,' buy one that is cheap. Avoid expensive lotions—they contain perfume that is painful to sex organs.)

Usually a woman asks her husband to spend a few minutes fondling her vagina, and then spend *many minutes fondling her clitoris*. The clitoris is located at the point where her inner lips meet. (page 46)

Wife, help your husband to find your clitoris. Just take his hand and move it to your clitoris. Show him the kind of fondling you prefer—whether gentle or firm.

Some women enjoy having both their clitoris and vagina fondled at the same time. So they ask their husband to slide a finger into the vagina while the palm of his hand rubs her clitoris. Other women, however, do not desire a finger in the vagina. They ask their husband to fondle their clitoris only.

It's good for a wife to talk freely!

The husband also should talk freely. He may say, "Please fondle my penis." Then after a minute he may tell her, "Stop now... I'm close to the point of ejaculating, but I don't want to ejaculate until I get inside you." Then she can let his penis rest while he continues fondling her. Later he may say, "Fondle me some more." And soon he may tell her again, "Stop fondling me, I'm close to ejaculating. Now do you want me to fondle you here . . . or there?"

Don't be silent during loveplay. Tell each other what you desire more of (and less of).

Free to enjoy: A husband and wife are free to do anything they like during loveplay.

As part of loveplay, some couples enjoy rubbing one another's body with body lotion. They rub each other from neck to toe, saving the sex organs for last. They may spend a long time like that—giving and receiving pleasure before entry.

Other couples choose to spend an hour together in a bath. When they get out of the bath, she may invite him to open her outer lips and look at the beauty of her clitoris, inner lips and vagina. This is one of the joys of marriage.

Some couples enjoy taking time to kiss each other's neck, ears, thighs . . . .

A husband and wife should never worry, "Are we doing this in a sinful way?"

There is nothing a husband and wife can do to each other that is a sin. No Bible-verse says, "A husband and his wife must not. . . ."

Of course, it would be a sin to have sex with someone who is not your husband/wife. Don't even *think* of that. (Matt. 5 28) But with your own husband/wife, nothing is sin. *You are free to do whatever both of you enjoy.*

But don't do anything that one of you doesn't like.

During loveplay, give your husband/wife pleasure in all the ways he/she likes. Tell each other what feels good. Talk. Don't hurry. Take time. Enjoy each other!

Every delightful pleasure, both old and new, I have saved for you. (Song of Songs 7 13)

Step Three
Enter

As loveplay continues, her husband will notice that her inner lips have increased in size. That shows she is very excited. And she will realise, "I'm so excited. I'm close to orgasm. Now is the time for my husband to enter me."

'Orgasm' means the feeling of highest excitement.

When a woman has an orgasm, she feels wonderful pleasure for about ten seconds. The pleasure begins in her clitoris and spreads to her whole body.

When a man has an orgasm, he also feels great pleasure for ten seconds. During his orgasm, a spoonful of white liquid shoots from his penis. In other words, he 'ejaculates.' After he ejaculates, he wants to stop all motion for at least a minute.

Enter at the right time

Husbands, you can help your wife to reach orgasm. How? Enter at the right time. Build her excitement until she is close to orgasm . . . then enter. If she is *close* before you enter, probably she will succeed in reaching orgasm after you enter.

Yes, continue loveplay until she says, "I'm excited…I think I'm near orgasm…please enter me now."

To enter, the husband moves his body over hers. He does not allow his weight to rest on her. Instead, his weight is on his knees and elbows. She uses her hand to put his penis into her vagina.

He must be careful not to cause her pain by entering too deeply. She will tell him how deep she prefers.

Enter . . . then wait one minute

After entry the danger is: He may ejaculate too soon. If he is not careful, he will ejaculate just a few seconds after entry. That is too soon because his wife needs time to reach her orgasm.

Men, here is advice that will help you: After you enter, *wait one minute* before you begin to move.

During that minute your excitement will fall. It's good for your excitement to fall because that will help you to avoid ejaculating too soon.

After the minute, begin your in-and-out motion. Since your excitement has decreased, probably you will be able to continue the motion for several minutes before you ejaculate. During those 'several minutes,' hopefully your wife will reach orgasm.

Her first, or same time, or him first?

Each time you have sex, there are three ways it may go.

Either a) she will have *her orgasm first,*

or b) they will have orgasms at the *same time,*

or c) he will have *his orgasm first.*

Let's look at each of those three.

a) her first. It's good if the wife reaches orgasm before her husband. While she is having hers, he enjoys watching her pleasure. Then he continues his in-and-out motion until he ejaculates. Although she has had her orgasm, his motion will not be painful to her.

b) same time. It's also good if they reach orgasm at the same time. Then they have the joy of giving pleasure as they are receiving it.

c) him first. It's not good if he has his orgasm first. Why? Because after he ejaculates, suddenly any motion is painful to his penis. So he stops moving. Then her excitement may fall. And if a woman's excitement falls, it's difficult to build it up again.

What can a husband do if he finds that he has ejaculated before she could reach orgasm?

Answer: He can help her excitement not to fall. How? Immediately after he ejaculates, he can begin using his fingers to fondle her clitoris (while his penis remains quiet in her vagina). Although his penis is not moving, his fingers can help her excitement to grow. After some minutes he will be able to move his penis without pain. Then he can continue moving in-and-out until she reaches orgasm.

Talking helps. When he ejaculates too soon, she may say, "Please help me to reach orgasm . . . love my clitoris with your fingers."

Or she may say, "Tonight I feel no need for an orgasm. If you need more orgasms, I'll gladly help you. Then let's fall asleep holding each other close."

When a wife doesn't reach orgasm, she may feel un-satisfied—but as she rests in her husband's arms, that unsatisfied feeling will slowly disappear.

How to make your sex better

In her letter Esther writes, "Before I have time to get excited, he enters me and ejaculates."

In other words, their sex is always 'him first.'

Here are three points that will help a husband and wife to succeed in having 'her first' or 'same time' orgasms.

◆ Love your husband/wife all day—not just in bed.

Don't be self-centred all day, and then sweet in bed. Instead, be careful to 'LOVE' your partner *all day*.

'LOVE' means talking with your partner like you talk with a friend...sharing joys and discussing problems.

'LOVE' means speaking kindly, even when he/she has made a mistake. 'LOVE' means helping one another by caring for the children together—instead of the wife doing it all. 'LOVE' means unselfish kindness.

Nobody wants to be fondled at night by a partner who has been un-loving all day. But if your partner has been sweet all day, how exciting the sex is at night!

◆ Control your thoughts.

Wife, during sex don't allow your mind to think about the washing and ironing you must do tomorrow. Your excitement will not grow unless you concentrate your thoughts on the joy of sex with your husband.

◆ Talk to each other.

During sex, both should talk, saying things like, "My orgasm is still far away...please touch me here...now my orgasm is starting...it's *great*...how can I help you?"

A husband may wonder, "Does she prefer *deep* entry, or not so deep?" How can he find out? *Talk to her.*

A wife may think, "I wish to try a new position, but maybe he doesn't want to try something new." How can she find out? *Talk to him.*

After her orgasm, she may say, "Let's see if we can both have another orgasm. Please keep moving...or love my clitoris with your fingers until I get another orgasm."

You are free to say such things. Why? *Because you are married.* (Gen. 2 ^{25}, Song of Songs 7 $^{7-13}$)

Step Four
Relax Afterwards

Many wives say, "After sex, my husband turns his back on me and goes to sleep. Then I find myself thinking, 'Does he love me?'"

The facts are: After ejaculating a man wants to sleep. But a woman is different. After sex she needs her husband to hold her and tell her a few more times, "I love you."

Listen, men. After sex don't go to sleep immediately. Spend more time telling her how you love her. When she is ready for sleep, the two of you can fall asleep together.

Sincere Christian couples enjoy sex much more than **half-hearted** Christian couples. Why? Because half-hearted Christians are selfish and unkind during the day, and that spoils their sex at night. Sincere Christians are careful all day to be kind and helpful. And then, when they get into bed, it's marvelous!

A Sex-Problem

Joel and Miriam went to a good Christian couple to get marriage counsel. Joel told them, "The problem in our marriage is sex. My wife doesn't like sex."

Miriam looked down at the floor, trying not to cry as she said, "My husband doesn't show love to me. He's nice to his mother and sisters, but not to me. When I try to talk with him, he says little or nothing. Then at night when I undress, he wants my body. But I can't enjoy sex because I feel unloved."

The couple discussed with them how a husband/wife should communicate and show kindness to each other.

After that, Miriam began to feel Joel's love . . . and their sex improved.

It wasn't a sex-problem. It was a love-problem.

In chapters 1 to 5 of this book, we explained *love* and *communication*. Perhaps you decided to skip those chapters and read this chapter first. Okay, we don't blame you for that. Sex is important. But knowing everything about sex will not help you unless you do the things explained in chapters 1 to 5.

So, go back now and read those chapters. And do them. Then your sex can become *really romantic!*

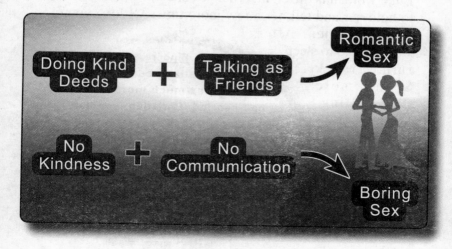

Chapter 8

First night after the wedding

Dear Bruce,

Your book, *"Love & Marriage"* showed me how to live. With the encouragement I got from that book, I've succeeded in remaining a virgin.

In three weeks I'm going to marry a marvellous girl. She promises that she is a virgin too. I'm very glad!

Yet I worry. How can I marry? I know too little about sex.

When I hear guys talk about sex, their talk is dirty stories. Once when I asked a question, they told me, "If you want to learn, go have sex with a woman who has experience."

I refuse to do that because I'm a Christian.

I would like you to give me holy information on sex. I'm sorry to ask you to write about this. I don't want to embarrass you. But the Bible says that a man must *"bring happiness to his wife."* (Deut. 24 5) Please tell me how to do that. Especially tell me what a man should do on his wedding night.

Yours in Christ,

Gideon

Dear Carol,

When I was age 12 a nice, Christian lady taught us girls every Sunday. She used the book *"Love & Marriage."* Then many of us girls promised, "I will honour God by remaining a virgin until I marry."

I have kept that promise.

Next month I'm going to marry a wonderful Christian man.

My problem is: After the wedding when my husband and I get into bed, I will not know what to do.

I believe that sex is a blessed wedding-gift from God. I'm looking forward to sex with my husband. But I worry because I don't know how to do it.

Yours faithfully,

Naomi

A bride and groom need knowledge about what to do on the wedding night. And they should receive that knowledge at the right time.

The right time is: About a week before the wedding—not sooner.

But don't young people need *months* to learn those things? No. This chapter tells everything. And to read this chapter takes an *hour*—not months.

Therefore, a young person should not receive this book until a week before his/her wedding. Again we say: Don't leave this book laying in places where young people may find it. Young people are responsible to wait for sex until marriage. If they start reading about sex too soon, waiting becomes more difficult.

When young people tell us, "I fear that I won't know what to do when I marry," we reply, "Don't worry. A week before your wedding you can get the knowledge you need by reading *Answers for your Marriage.*"

To churches we say, "It's good to give each young man and young lady a copy of this book (one week before they marry.)"

Information for a bride and groom

After the wedding when a virgin bride and groom enter the bedroom, their hearts are full of joy. This is the time they have been waiting for. Before marriage they were tempted to have sex, but they said 'no.' They obeyed God. They waited for this day. Now it has come!

They will enjoy sex more because they know, "It's right for us to begin sex now. God approves, and our families approve."

Yet, in their minds are questions.

She wants sex with her husband; but she asks herself, "Will it hurt?"

He wonders, "If I fail to satisfy her, will she doubt that I'm a real man?"

Her attitude should be, "You must not worry if I don't reach orgasm tonight. I won't think there is something wrong with you. As days and months pass, we will learn to satisfy one another. And we will enjoy the learning."

His attitude should be, "I'll be careful not to hurt you. I won't just think of my own pleasure. I will help you to enjoy it."

If they have those attitudes, their fears will disappear, and they will feel free to talk—even telling each other what hurts, and what feels good.

How beautiful it is when two virgins begin having sex after the wedding!

It's another story for the young people who decide to disobey God. For example, when Grace was only 16, she had her first sex with a guy named Sam. During loveplay Sam feared, "If I fail to do sex well, she will tell her friends that I'm a lousy lover." In fact, both of them were afraid of appearing ignorant. So they tried to act like experts. After a brief time of loveplay, Sam entered and ejaculated. The next day Grace could not stop asking herself:

How many people will he tell?
Did he give me a sex-disease?
Condoms sometimes fail. What if
I'm pregnant?
Will any man ever love me, or will
they just use *my body* like Sam did?

Sex before marriage is not beautiful. Humans cannot find true joy by breaking the law of their Creator.

Happy are the people who obey God by saying 'no' to sex before marriage. On their wedding night, the groom is glad that his bride has not experienced other men. And she is happy that he never had sex with other girls.

> *A virgin bride and virgin groom have the very special joy of learning together from no one except each other.*

Abner told us, "Next month is my wedding, but my future-bride has had sex with other guys, and I've had sex with other girls. We wish we were virgins. What can we do?"

Answer, "Repent. Accept Christ as your Lord. He will forgive your sins. He will help your marriage. Yet, your past sexual sins will still cause some problems in your marriage. So, encourage your children to love God, and remain virgins until marriage." [See pages 93-94 and 124.]

Preparing for first sex

After your wedding when the two of you are alone in a bedroom, we suggest that you begin with a simple prayer saying, "Dear Lord, with joy we will spend the years of our lives working for you together. And in our marriage we want to be unselfishly kind to each other."

Don't worry…you will *enjoy* this evening. Relax. Talk in a carefree way.

Lock the door. Then enjoy undressing each other. For a new husband and wife who are virgins, undressing in front of each other is a special joy. Don't hurry. Spend time kissing, then each of you can take a piece of clothing off the other, and after more kissing, remove another piece.

Don't hide in the dark. Enjoy seeing each other's body in the light. This is God's gift to each husband and wife.

> The man and his wife were both naked,
> and they were not ashamed. (Gen. 2 25)

First loveplay

As explained on page 47, a couple should begin loveplay by fondling each other's *upper* body. Then, after some minutes, the wife will become excited and move his hand down to her vagina. As he fondles her, he should freely ask, "Do you prefer that I fondle you here or there . . . like this, or like that?"

She should tell him each time he does something that helps her excitement to grow. This will encourage him.

His wife will *not* be thinking, "I wish he had practised on other girls so he would know what to do."

Instead, she will be telling herself,

> **"I love being his only sex-partner.
> I'm glad he never did this to anyone else!"**

On their wedding night, a couple should continue loveplay for a *long* time (30 minutes or more). Then they must try to decide: Should he enter now? Is she close to orgasm, or does she still need more loveplay?

They may be unsure. The wife may think, "I feel excited, but I don't know if I'm close to orgasm."

And as her husband feels her sex organs, he may wonder, "Have her 'inner lips' increased in size? Should I enter now?"

On their wedding night Reuben and Bernice did not spend enough time in loveplay. He thought, "She is near orgasm." So he entered her. But in fact, she was still *far* from it. The result was: Reuben ejaculated before she could reach orgasm…then her excitement fell…and she did not have an orgasm that night. Was that a big problem? No. They enjoyed loving each other, and they both learned something about when to enter.

On Philip and Anna's wedding night, he waited too long before entering. He was still fondling the area outside her vagina (around her clitoris) when she began having an orgasm! So he continued fondling her clitoris for a minute until her orgasm was over. Then he entered her vagina and ejaculated. Later he asked, "How did you reach orgasm when I was fondling the area *outside* your vagina? I mean, with nothing inside your vagina, how…?"

As they discussed it, Philip realised: *It's the clitoris (not the vagina) that brings a woman to orgasm.* [page 46]

As years pass marriage grows better!

On your wedding night, don't be worrying, "Will we satisfy each other on our first night?"

Just enjoy your wedding night—even if the bride does not reach orgasm. Enjoy touching and fondling each other. Remember: The wedding night is just a beginning. It's the beginning of a life-time of learning how to give each other pleasure. In the days ahead, you will learn how to build each other's excitement. You will learn how to satisfy one another. And when you have been married ten years, you will still be learning, and your sex will still be growing more pleasurable and more fun. (Prov. 5 18-19)

The **'Hymen'** is a piece of skin that covers the vagina. It has a round hole in it.

A girl may have a 'thin hymen,' or 'thick hymen,' or 'broken hymen.'

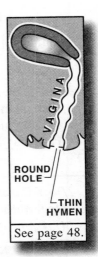

1) Thin hymen. Most girls have a thin hymen with a hole of about 2 cm diameter.

A man's hard penis is 3 or 4 cm diameter, and so the hymen will stretch or break during first-sex. This may cause a little pain and bleeding.

Girls, do this: Wait...have your first-sex with your husband on your wedding night. As he enters, your hymen will break. Don't worry. The pain will be small compared to the joy of being loved by your husband.

And as your hymen breaks, your husband will be thinking, "I'm glad to know that I'm the first and only man to enter my sweet bride."

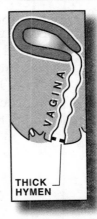

2) Thick hymen. A few girls (about 10%) have a thick hymen. On her wedding night, a girl with a thick hymen may find that her husband's penis cannot enter her vagina. In that case, she can stretch her hymen. This may take 5 days. Each day she spends two minutes stretching it with her fingers. At first she will be able to put in only one finger. After 3 days she will be able to put in two, and after 5 days, three fingers. Then her husband will succeed in entering. Although he had to wait 5 days, he will be glad to know, "My bride never had sex before."

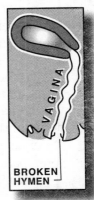

3) Broken hymen. A girl's hymen will break if she has sex.

Listen all girls. Many things on earth change, but one thing never changes: On a man's wedding night, he likes to find that his bride has an unbroken hymen. Then he knows, "No man's penis ever entered my bride. She waited for me."

Listen all mothers. While your daughter is still young, begin telling her about her hymen.

Simply say, "Sex is for marriage. Don't have sex before marriage. On your wedding night, your husband will be glad if he finds that your hymen is unbroken."

In many cultures, mothers or grandmothers inspect a girl's hymen now and then—to be sure it's still unbroken. This may help a girl to wait for marriage.

Dear Carol,
My wedding is next week. I fear first-sex. Everyone tells me,
"During first-sex a girl feels pain, and she bleeds."
Lois

Dear Lois,

Don't worry. It's true that a girl may feel some pain and bleed a little during first-sex. She bleeds because her hymen breaks. But you don't need to fear sex with your husband. Just think like this:

It's good if my hymen breaks on my wedding night. Then my husband will realise:

No other man ever entered me.
He himself broke my hymen.
I belong to him.
He belongs to me.
(Song of Songs 6[3])

How to enter

After enjoying loveplay for a long time, the bride may say, "I'm so excited; I think it's time for entry." Then she can use her hands to move his penis to her vagina.

If she touches the *end* of his penis with *dry* hands, it will be painful to him. So she should wet her hands with body lotion.

As he enters, her hymen will break, and she may feel some pain.

Listen, husband. Enter <u>slowly</u>. Then she will feel <u>less</u> pain.

Problems you may have

◆ **"I can't enter."** Husband, if you fail to enter because her hymen is thick, let her use her fingers to enlarge it. That may take some minutes or some days. Then you will be able to enter.

◆ **"Will his penis be too big?"** Wife, don't worry. Don't tell yourself, "His penis is so large in diameter, it will always be painful to me." The fact is: Your hymen will break during first sex...after that your vagina will easily accept his penis...no matter if it is small or large.

◆ **"He enters too deeply."** Husband, be careful not to cause your wife pain by entering too deeply. Your wife can show you how deep she prefers. Many women find that sex is *most* exciting when he enters only 6 to 8 cm.

◆ **"During sex my vagina is painful."** Worry can cause the vagina-muscle to become tight and painful. Therefore, wife, avoid worry. Relax.

Listen, men. If sex is painful for your wife, be extra gentle. If she still feels pain, tell her, "Let's not have sex now. I can wait. Next time, as you begin to relax, it won't be painful."

Saying that shows *love*. *'Love'* means: Being more concerned about her needs than my needs.

◆ **"My penis is small."** Men, if your penis is small, don't worry. The truth is: A man with a small penis can satisfy his wife just as well as a man with a large one. A large penis has no advantage. A small penis has no disadvantage. *It makes no difference.* [page 96]

After entry, help her to reach orgasm

When a husband enters his wife, the next step is: They begin doing all they can to help *her* to reach orgasm *before he has an orgasm*. That means, they try to build her excitement, and reduce his.

To reduce his excitement, after entering he should not move for one minute. During that minute, they can build her excitement in three ways:

1) While his penis is motionless in her vagina, he can fondle her clitoris with his fingers.

2) She can rotate her hips. During that first minute, it's better to rotate than to move in-and-out. Why? Because in-and-out motion makes a man ejaculate. But if she rotates (and avoids in-and-out), she will grow excited without exciting him.

3) She can squeeze his penis with her vagina. The vagina muscle is called the 'PC muscle.' [page 162] As she squeezes his penis with her vagina, it won't excite him much, but it will excite her.

After one minute, his excitement should be low, and hers high. Then he can begin moving in-and-out.

Since his excitement is low, probably he will be able to continue moving without ejaculating too soon.

If she wishes, she may do this: As his penis moves out, she squeezes her vagina…as he moves in, she relaxes her vagina. Some wives enjoy this and find that it helps them to reach orgasm.

When her orgasm begins, she tells him. Then he stops holding himself back, and probably he will ejaculate during her orgasm, or soon after.

It's nice when it happens like that—but on the *first* night, things don't always go that well. Instead, one of the following three things may happen:

a) Husband has an orgasm before he enters

Sometimes a husband accidentally ejaculates while his wife is fondling him during loveplay. That is not a sin. In fact, they can enjoy it. [Abigail, page 105]

However, a man prefers to ejaculate inside her vagina. So, before entry as they are fondling each other, he may tell his wife, "Wait, I'm nearly going to ejaculate...don't fondle me...let me cool for a few minutes."

After those few minutes she can fondle him again, until he tells her, "Wait, I need to cool again."

In loveplay, he should fondle her *all the time*.

But she should *fondle him...let him cool...fondle him...let him cool....* That will help him not to ejaculate too quickly after he enters her. And it will make his ejaculation extra enjoyable.

b) Wife has an orgasm before he enters her

Sometimes a wife has an orgasm during loveplay while he is fondling her clitoris. That is not a sin. They can enjoy it. But next time he should enter sooner so that she reaches orgasm after entry. That brings more pleasure.

c) Husband has an orgasm during entry

He may accidentally ejaculate while entering. Then any kind of motion will be painful to him. So he will need to tell his wife, "Don't move for a couple of minutes—I just ejaculated."

During those couple of minutes he can fondle her clitoris with his fingers. That will help her excitement to grow. When he is able to begin moving, hopefully she will reach orgasm. Then he may have another one.

We will enjoy learning from each other

Not many couples succeed in giving each other orgasms on their first night. In most cases, the husband has some orgasms...the wife has none.

Therefore, on your first night, don't be discouraged. Wife, don't tell yourself, "My body is under-sexed." Husband, don't say, "My body can't satisfy a woman." Instead, remind each other that:

As husband and wife, we will learn to satisfy each other. Learning will be fun. In all the years ahead, we will be careful to continue satisfying each other. And we will never have sex with anyone else.

If we talk freely, we will learn faster

If your sex isn't very satisfying during the first days of marriage, don't worry. As months pass, you will learn how to please each other. Learning takes time.

One thing that will help you is: Talk to each other.

Couples who talk freely
learn faster.

Seth and Eunice learned quickly. Why? Because they realised, *"Since we are married, we may speak to each other freely about sex."*

But Phinehas has not yet learned to satisfy his wife. He tells himself, "I'm a man. I know how to do sex." But he doesn't know what a clitoris is. And he never says to his wife, "Show me where you wish me to fondle you."

His wife has <u>never</u> said, "Please wet your fingers and fondle me here, on my clitoris...yes, that's nice, you wonderful husband."

She thinks, "A *Christian* wife must not speak to her husband about such things."

The truth is:
A husband and wife are free
to talk with each other about sex.
Why? Because they are married.
(Mark 10 [8])

How to enjoy sex

We asked people in Europe, Africa, Asia... *"How could your husband/wife help you to enjoy sex more?"*

Husbands said: *I would enjoy sex more if my wife would:*

✓ let me see her body with no clothes.

✓ sometimes invite me for sex (instead of me always being the one to invite her).

✓ not think, "Since my husband made me angry, I will punish him by being half-hearted in bed."

✓ stop saying, "Christian women shouldn't enjoy sex."

✓ talk to me during loveplay, telling me what she likes.

Wives said: *I would enjoy sex more if my husband would:*

✓ be a friend to me, so that I will feel free to talk with him about everything... including sex.

✓ never have sex with anyone but me. I hate the thought of any other woman or girl in bed with my husband!

✓ reduce suspicion. Tell me where he is going, and who he is with.

✓ do sex in new ways—not the same every time.

✓ be kind to me. I can't feel romantic if he is rude all day and then sweet in bed.

✓ communicate. I feel close to him when he asks for my opinion on decisions, and we discuss our ideas.

✓ be a better father to our children. I can't feel sexy when he shows little interest in our kids.

✓ invite me to pray with him each morning. When we pray together, I feel close to him and to God.

✓ tell me that he loves me, and say it at any time—not just in bed.

Chapter 9

Be a good Dad/Mum to your kids

Carol and I thank God that our kids love Christ. Our daughter is married to a pastor. Our son and his wife serve God by inviting neighbours to their home for Bible study.

In this chapter we will see what the Bible says about how to raise children.

Gideon: Today most parents work hard to buy nice things for their kids; yet when those kids become teenagers, many turn to beer, sex and drugs.

My wife and I have three children (ages 3 to 8). How can we help them to grow into respectful teenagers and adults?

Dear Gideon,

Spend time with your children. Talk with them. Show them love. Teach them Bible stories. (Psa. 78)

As our kids were growing up, Carol and I often gave each of them a hug, and said, "I love you." And nearly every day either Carol or I told them a Bible story. We tried to tell the story in an exciting way so they would be glad to listen. Sometimes we told it while sitting at the dinner table, or while going for a walk.

After the Bible story, usually I

A child must reach the point of saying:

"God is good. I'm not good. I'm sinful.
Jesus is God.
He died for my sins.
Today I take Jesus.
Now he will be with me every day here on earth, and I will live with him forever."

said something like, "Kids, let me tell you what happened today to one of my students who cheated on his exam."

Then Carol would say something like, "When I was a girl, I got into trouble when I told a lie about . . . ."

As we told such stories, our kids realised, "Dad and Mum love us...they want us to stay out of trouble."

So, Gideon, spend time with your kids. Wash the car together. Go for walks. Tell them Bible stories. And tell them true stories about people whose lives were spoiled because they turned from God. Also tell stories of people you know who are finding great joy in serving Christ.

Make your stories *interesting*. Use some sad stories, and some happy ones that will make them laugh. Soon your kids will be begging you, "Please, Dad and Mum, tell us another story!"

> **God says,
> "Teach my laws
> to your children.
> Teach them when you
> sit in your house,
> and when you walk
> along the road, and
> when you lie down,
> and when you rise up."**
> (Deut. 6 6-7)

One day a young man told me, "Bruce, each time I visit your home, I'm amazed at how you talk with your kids. When I was a boy, my father said nothing to me except, 'Take this cup to the kitchen. Stop making noise.'"

I replied, "Obey Deut. 6 6-7. Talk with your children 'when you sit in your house, and when you walk, and when you lie down, and when you rise up.'"

Today many parents spend too little time with their kids. Many Mums and Dads are overly busy earning money. As parents, they should say to each other,

Let's find ways to spend more time with our kids — even if it means we earn less money.

What happens when parents spend too little time with their kids? Do their kids say, "Mum and Dad, please spend time with us?" No, kids don't say that. But they secretly wish for Mum and Dad to show interest in them. Their hearts feel *empty*.

TV or Dad

The average child spends 2 <u>hours</u> per day watching TV, and 2 <u>minutes</u> per day talking with his/her Dad.

When they become teenagers, they may use beer or sex to try to satisfy their empty feeling.

When I was a teacher in Swaziland, another teacher told me, "Bruce, in addition to teaching day-school, you should teach evening-school. Then each month you'll get an extra cheque. And tell your wife to get a job. Look at my new furniture. I bought it with the money I got from teaching evening-school."

But I told Carol, "If you get a job, and if I teach evening-school, what will happen to our evening 'story time'? No, let's continue spending time with our kids, no matter if our furniture is old."

Hug your kids. Have fun with them. Tell them exciting Bible stories. Talk with them. Listen to their problems and joys. Pray with them. (Psalm 78)

Also love each other as husband and wife. (Eph. 5 $^{25\text{-}33}$ and 1 Pet. 3 $^{1\text{-}7}$)

Dad and Mum love each other, and they love us. We can feel safe.

Elizabeth: At university my psychology professor said, "Parents should never use a stick on kids." What do you say?

Dear Elizabeth,

The Bible says: Don't fail to correct your child.
Punish him with a stick.
It will save his soul from death.
(Prov. 23 $^{13\text{-}14}$)

There is a *right* time and a *wrong* time to use a stick.

The right time: If you tell your small son, "Take this spoon to the kitchen," but he chooses not to do it, fetch a little stick. He knew what to do, but he chose not to obey.

The wrong time: Don't use a stick when the child has forgotten to do something, or made a mistake. For example, if a child accidentally breaks a dish, you can make him do some extra work to pay for the dish (so he learns to be more careful), but don't go for a stick. Why? Because he didn't choose to disobey. It was an accident.

Never shake a child.
Never hit him on the head.
The safe place to spank a child is on the buttocks.
Never beat a child hard.
A <u>small</u> stick on the <u>buttocks</u>…that's enough to remind a child to obey.

Austin: When I was a kid, I *feared* my father. He over-used the stick.
   Now I'm a leader in the church, and I want to be a good father to my kids. Please advise me.

Dear Austin,
   Enjoy your children. Play ball with them. Laugh with them. Tell them exciting stories of great men and women of the Bible.
   If your small child speaks to you without respect, say to him, "My child, if you don't learn to respect, you will have endless troubles at school and with employers. Because I love you, I must give you two whacks with this little stick, just to remind you to show respect." (Proverbs 13 24 and 29 17)
   Then use the stick *lightly* on his *buttocks*.

> A man who is a church-leader should also be a good father to his children. (1 Tim. 3 4, 5, 12, Titus 1 6)

> **Listen all parents: Praise your children.** **Praise more often than you punish.**
> **Every day be careful to notice the things each child does well. Then tell him/her,**
> ***"You did that well."***
>   **Children need praise.**

Philip: The Bible says the husband is 'head.' Doesn't that mean my wife is like one of my children, and so I must discipline her like I discipline my children?

Dear Philip,

No. Don't discipline your wife. God says *two* things: 1) You are 'head.' 2) Your wife is your 'partner.' Since she is your 'partner,' the two of you should discuss issues as two adults. She is not a child. You don't discipline her.

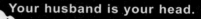

Your wife is your partner.   **Your husband is your head.**

Think of your wife's needs. She is physically weaker. Treat her as your partner. If you treat her right, nothing will hinder your prayers.
(1 Peter 3 7)

The husband is head of the wife. Wife, submit to your husband, like the church submits to Christ. Husband, love your wife, like Christ...
(Eph. 5 23-24)

When a man and wife disagree on things like, "Which furniture should we buy?" or "Where should we build our house?" sometimes the husband may decide to say, "Since you are my partner, let's do this your way."

Other times he may say, "I hear what you say, but in this case let's go with my suggestion." Then the wife should submit to him as head.

Caleb: My children learn about Jesus in Sunday school, but how can I see if they are really Christians?

Dear Caleb,

Take time to ask each one, "My child, if you stand before God and he asks you, 'Why should I allow you to enter heaven?' what answer could you give?"

Perhaps he/she will reply, *"The only reason I can enter heaven is: Jesus suffered for my sins. And I chose to trust him as my Lord and Saviour."* That answer is correct. That child is a Christian.

> **Even as a child you knew the holy Bible. It tells you how to be saved.**
> (2 Tim. 3 [15])

Or perhaps he/she will reply, "I hope I can enter heaven since I do good things."

That answer is <u>not</u> correct. So you should say, "My child, we all have sinned. We can't remove our sins by doing 'good things.' Our only hope is: Jesus died for our sins. My child, let's pray now. If you wish, you can tell Jesus, 'Today I choose to stop trusting my good deeds, and to begin trusting your death on the cross.' Then, my child, you will be a Christian, on the road to heaven."

David: How can we teach our kids to serve God?

Dear David,

Carol and I remember when we moved from one town to another in Swaziland. Soon our kids told us, "We don't like this town. We have no friends here."

Carol and I replied, "Honestly, we too feel sad to be in this place with no relatives or friends. Let's pray about it."

Together we thanked God for being with us, and we promised to continue working for him, no matter what.

God gave us nine good (but often difficult) years there. On the day we left, dozens of friends came to the airport to say good-bye. Some of them we had led to faith in Christ. After we entered the plane, a Swazi man told us, "Never before have I seen so many people crying in an airport. Your family has so many friends of all races. Why are you leaving? If I had friends like that, I'd stay!"

Later our kids said to us, "Remember nine years ago we were saying, 'We have no friends.' Then we prayed!"

It's good to serve God!

Abel: Last night as our family watched TV together, we saw a girl go to a hotel with a married man . . . but no one got into trouble . . . no AIDS, no pregnancy. TV made it look fun, with no bad-results.

How can we teach our kids the fact that:

In real life, sin brings trouble?

Dear Abel,

Spend little or no time watching TV. Spend much time talking with your kids about the Bible and 'real life.'

When our kids were teenagers, one day Carol invited Dan and his wife, Mary, to have dinner with us. They were not Christians, and we wanted to begin encouraging them to trust Christ.

As our kids were sitting at the table with us, Mary said, "Sorry we arrived late. My husband came late from work. I think he's playing with his secretary."

Dan shouted, "I was not. When will you *trust* me?"

"How can I *trust* you?" she shouted back. "In the past you've chased girls. You can't deny that!"

Carol and I felt sorry that our kids heard all that.

But the next day as we discussed it with our kids, they realised: *In real life sin brings trouble.*

The following year we were all glad when Dan and Mary turned to Christ and were baptised.

Another day a friend named Esther came to our home and said, "Let's celebrate! Exactly one year ago I accepted Christ. *And this has been the best year of my life!*"

As we were rejoicing, our kids asked, "Auntie Esther, why was this your best year?"

She replied, "Before I took Christ, my life was just going to discos, drinking, getting home late, feeling terrible in the morning, going to work, then back to discos, more drinking . . . what a lousy life! But since I accepted Christ, I have real friends, purpose for living, and eternal life!"

From such talks, our kids grew to realise:

Sin may look fun, but God's way is best.

Timothy: Six years ago when our first child was born, my wife quit her job. She says, "Children need a full-time mother."

Some people laugh at her and say she is lazy. To me, she is a great wife and mother.

Dear Timothy,

This is Carol writing. I'm glad your wife spends time with her kids. I did that too. I said 'no' to a job. As a result, we never had money for an expensive car/house. But I feel good that I invested so much time in our kids.

Some mothers say, "A good job is *more fulfilling* than raising kids."

But I say,

"The *most fulfilling* job on earth
is the job of being a good mother."

Today a growing number of women are deciding to be full-time mothers. Recently newspapers reported that Sandie (a famous fashion model) quit her job...why?...to spend more time with her kids.

Sandie says, "Last year my husband and I agreed that I should quit work and give time to our kids. When I was working, I only had a few hours each day with my kids. Now I have time to listen to their problems, pray with them, and do enjoyable things with them."

Note: At church, Sandie and her husband teach parents, *"How a family can live on the husband's salary...so the wife can be a full-time mother."*

Of course, not every woman can quit her job. Some women have no choice—they must work. God will help them to find time to spend with their kids.

But sometimes a mother chooses to work even though her husband has a job. She works because she wants to buy 'nice things.' She hires a girl to care for her children, but the girl cannot give them mother-love. When those children become teenagers, they may get into so much trouble that their parents will say, "The 'nice things' we bought are not that nice. How we wish we could turn the clock back 15 years and spend more time with our kids!"

So, Timothy, you and your wife are doing well. *No matter if you are not able to buy 'nice things,' you will never look back and say, "We are sorry we spent so much time with our kids."*

Joshua: What should I teach my kids about *giving* to God?

Dear Joshua,

Teach them (mainly by example) to do four things:

1) Give with joy. God loves a person who gives joyfully. (2 Corinth. 9 [7])	**3) Give to people who go to far places and start churches.** I always have a burning desire to preach in places where people have not yet heard of Christ. (Rom. 15 [20])
2) Give to 'elders' who teach the Bible diligently. Elders who work hard teaching the Bible should receive money from believers. (1 Corinth. 9 [14], 1 Tim. 5 [17-18])	**4) Give to people in need.** If you have two shirts, give one to him who has none. (Luke 3 [11])

When our kids were young, sometimes they said, "Dad and Mum, you give too much money to church—that's why we don't have nice toys."

We feared they would grow up to be people who hate to give. Yet we continued giving. And we continued teaching them verses that tell us to give.

By age 16 they were giving their own money that they had worked hard to earn. And today they are still generous givers.

It's good to be a family that gives!

Be a family that gives.

Mark: Should Christian men be involved in Sunday School, or should we leave that to women who are gifted at teaching children?

Dear Mark,

Boys like to have a Christian *man* teaching Sunday School. Especially *fatherless* boys need good, male teachers.

Therefore, Sunday Schools should have both **male and female** teachers.

When I started teaching Sunday School, I had no idea how to do it. But now I love teaching kids.

God gives the gift of teaching children to some women and to some men. Anyone who has the gift should use it.

If you have no gift for teaching, you can still help in Sunday School. How? Plan a 'Saturday of Fun.' Invite kids from church and kids from town. It will be a great day for kids [especially fatherless kids] to meet men and women who love Christ and love children.

In addition to Sunday School, there are other ways to help kids. When my own kids were about age ten, I used to tell them, "On Saturday let's go for a fun walk in a rural area. Each of you can bring a friend who has no father. We will make a fire and roast meat. Then I'll tell an exciting Bible story. We will enjoy the day!"

Satan tells me, "Bruce, you don't have time for kids; you have important work to do."

But God likes to *"turn the hearts of fathers to their children."* (Malachi 4 [6])

Kids need a father's love.

John: If a son or daughter of age 20 is living in sin, is that the fault of the child or the parents?

Dear John,

Sometimes it's both. When Eli's sons did evil, God punished both Eli and his sons. Why Eli? Because he had not even tried to be a good father. (1 Sam. 3 [13])

Sometimes it's not the parents' fault — it's the child's fault. For example, Samuel's sons did evil, but God never said that Samuel was a bad father. (1 Sam. 8 [3])

Therefore we tell parents, "Be an example to your kids. Behave as a Christian should. Encourage your kids to accept Christ. But if your child of age 20 says, 'I've decided; I don't want Jesus,' that will be his choice — not yours. Since you were careful to be a good parent, God will not punish you. But pray for your child, and continue showing him/her the way." (Ezekiel 18 [1-32])

Bernice: I'm a single mother of three children. My son (age 17) tells me, "I'm tired of your rules. You always want to know where I'm going, and you tell me what time I must be home. Look, I'm an adult!"

Yesterday he came home with a girl. He wanted to spend the night with her in his bedroom. I refused. Then he shouted swear-words at me.

I've done my best to be a good parent. What can I do?

Dear Bernice,

Tell your son, "The reason I have rules is: *I love you.* As long as you stay in this home, you must obey the home-rules."

Bernice, ask the people of your church for help.

> **Churches should love to help single mothers.**

Our Advice to all Parents Worldwide

If you have not been a good parent, do this: Ask Christ to forgive you. Then start today to show love to your kids and pray for them.

Prayer does much! When our two kids were ages 16 and 17, one Saturday I decided to spend the morning in prayer. I like to walk while I pray, so I left the house and began praying quietly as I walked. I prayed for people in Somalia and Libya who have not yet heard of eternal life in Christ. I prayed for people in France and England who have left the church. Then I prayed for Christians...*may they arise and spread the Good News*.

After a couple of hours I went home for a few minutes to see if my family was okay. There Carol told me, "Sue talked rudely to me. She's at school now, but when she comes home, you need to confront her."

As I drank tea, I said to our son, "Bob, didn't you say that you want to start teaching Sunday School? Today you could phone the man in charge and ask if he needs you."

Bob said nothing. I could see he didn't feel like phoning anyone.

Then I continued my prayer-walk. By now I realised, "For the next hour I must pray for my wife and kids!"

When I finally returned home, there was Sue, hugging her mother…crying…and saying, "Sorry."

And Bob was studying his Bible. "I phoned him," Bob said with a smile. "Now I must prepare a lesson."

That day I told myself, "God *works* through prayer!" I'm sure God worked not only in my family, but also in Libya, England, and the other nations I prayed for. Yet I learned to pray for my *family first*.

Yes, let's all pray for our kids like Jesus prayed for Simon Peter:

"Satan wants to have you, Simon,
 but I have prayed for you…" (Luke 22 31-32)

And let's pray for all nations, as Jesus told us to:

"Pray that the Lord will send workers to his fields." (Matt. 9 38)

Letters
from people with problems

Nathan: Last month the man who stays in the flat above us chased away his wife and kids. Then he married his girlfriend. Actually, this is his third divorce and re-marriage.

My wife and I fear that our teenage children may be influenced by this guy's awful behaviour.

Dear Nathan,

At first he may appear to be happy with his new wife. But as months pass, he will begin to see her faults. Then he will tell himself, "This woman no longer excites me. I wanted to begin an exciting new life, but nothing's new."

Perhaps he will begin looking for a new woman; one who will unselfishly care for him (while he selfishly cares for himself), and one who is always sexy (no matter how badly he treats her).

As he goes from woman to woman, he will leave behind many ex-wives who feel terribly hurt. And his children will wish for a father who loves them.

Nathan, as your children notice all that, they will realise:

A man who lives in sin never finds long-lasting joy. And he brings much sorrow to his kids/wives.

Listen, Nathan. Your job is:
1) Pray for him every day.
2) Be kind to him. Find ways to help him. Show love.
3) After he begins to trust you as a friend, tell him how to receive forgiveness, a new life, and heaven. [See page 27, "How I became a Christian." Also pages 128-136.]

Philip: My wife and I have 3 children. The youngest is from our marriage. The eldest I got from a girlfriend before I married. The other one is my wife's. She got pregnant from her boyfriend before I met her.

Last year our neighbour invited us to a "Bring-a-Friend" service at church. There my wife and I repented. We asked Jesus to forgive our sins, and we accepted him as our Lord.

The problem is: My wife still loves the father of her first child. Today I found this note from her to him.

> *Darling, I think of you day and night. When can you visit me? I wrote to you, but you didn't reply.*

When I asked her about it, she said, "How can you complain about my ex-boyfriend? Don't you still meet your ex-girlfriend?"

It's true. I still feel love for my ex, and I meet her for sex. My wife does the same for her ex. So our marriage is rotten.

Dear Philip,

God has two big commands for both of you:

Command 1: Love your wife/husband. Right now both of you feel love for your ex's. Do this: *Stop feeding* those feelings. That means, stop writing to your ex's, and stop meeting them.

At the same time, *feed* your feelings for one another. How? Choose to be kind in your words and actions.

As you, Philip, choose to have no romantic communication with your ex, your feelings for her will decrease. And as you choose to be kind/helpful to your wife, your feelings for her will grow.

Similarly, as your wife tells herself, "I will not write to my ex; instead I will do nice things for my husband," her feelings for you will grow.

Command 2: No sex outside marriage. Enjoy sex with your wife/husband.

I am yours. You are mine. (Song of Songs 6^3)

Never have sex with anyone else. God says:

> **Run away from sex outside marriage. Sex-sin is different from other sins. Sex-sin affects your body...it is a sin against your own body.**
>
> **Your body is the temple of the Holy Spirit. He lives in you. Your body does not belong to you. It belongs to God. He bought you at a price.✝ Therefore, honour God with your body.** (1 Corinth. 6 $^{18-20}$)
>
> **The temptations that come to you are no greater than other people have. God will not let anyone tempt you above your strength. Each time you are tempted, he will make a way for you to escape.** (1 Corinth. 10 ^{13})

The above verses say that you can choose to have victory over sex-sin...yes..."each time you are tempted, he will make a way for you to escape."

So, you can choose victory if you want to.

Remember: God is no fool. Your life will go better if you choose to fear him. (Ecc. 8 $^{11-13}$ and Gal. 6 ^{7})

Joel: I'm a single guy (age 29). I'm madly in love with a recently married woman. She and I sing in a choir at church. I try to wipe her out of my mind. But whenever I see her, I die with love.

Yesterday I went to her home and told her, "I want to stop feeling love for you." But then I couldn't stop myself from kissing her. She responded by kissing me deeply.

Today I went back just to tell her, "Sorry I kissed you." Then we ended up kissing passionately again.

How can I stop loving her? The only plan I can think of is: *I must have sex with her just one time.* That will cool my desire for her body.

Dear Joel,

The Word of God says:

> Can a man hold fire against his chest?
> It is equally dangerous to sleep with
>   another man's wife.
> God will punish whoever touches her.
>   (Prov. 6 $^{27,\ 29}$)

Listen, Joel. Never again enter her house. And if your desire for her continues, leave that choir.

> Run away from the lust
> that young men often have. (2 Tim. 2 22)

Joel, your plan is: "Have sex with his wife once." When you say that, we must say, "We doubt you are a Christian."

You attend church, but have you ever decided to become a Christian? Have you ever told God, "I deserve hell...but today I take Christ."?

We encourage you to do that now...like this:

A PRAYER TO BECOME A CHRISTIAN

Lord Jesus, I'm sinful. I deserve to suffer for my sins, but you came to earth and suffered in my place. Today I take you as my Saviour. When I die, you will take me to heaven — not because of any good I do, but just because you died for the sins I have done.
Starting today, you are my Lord.
I want to obey you and serve you.

David: My brother is miserable because his wife commits adultery. Do women commit adultery for the same reasons men do it . . . or do women have their own reasons?
How can my wife and I avoid adultery?

Dear David,
Here are the main reasons people do adultery.

1) Feeling of Love.
A woman may ask herself, "Does my husband still love me? Long ago he liked to spend time with me, and talk with me. What a marvellous feeling I had back then! I wish I had that feeling now."

Then a neighbour man begins talking to her. Suddenly she has that feeling again — the feeling of *"Someone loves me."* And she is tempted to give sex to the man who gives her that feeling.

To avoid adultery: Husband, love your wife! Love her not only with sex, but especially with friendly communication. If she feels you really love her, she will not hunger to receive love from another guy. [See pages 7-24.]

2) New Sex. While women are tempted by a new 'Feeling of Love,' men are tempted by 'New Sex.'

Men think, "Wouldn't it be fun to have sex with someone *new!*" Do *Christian* men feel that temptation? Yes. And God commands us to say, 'No.' (Titus 2 12)

To avoid adultery: Wife, make the sex in your marriage exciting. Don't let it become half-hearted. Do sex in new ways. Keep sex so exciting that your husband will not be strongly tempted to look for 'New Sex.' A man who has a Mercedes at home is less tempted to steal a bicycle.

3) Appreciation. A husband or wife may feel tempted to have sex with someone who, *"enjoys listening to me, and likes the way I think, and says I'm intelligent and nice-looking."*

We all need that kind of appreciation.

There are many sinful women who know how to show appreciation to another woman's husband. And often a sinful man shows zero appreciation to his own wife, but speaks so sweetly to another man's wife . . . in the hope of talking her into adultery.

To avoid adultery: Show appreciation to your own husband/wife. You may think, "At home I receive no appreciation—why should I give any?"
Answer: Because God commands you to love and appreciate your own husband/wife. And God will help you do that. [See pages 29-34.]

4) Everyone's doing it. As they watch TV, some people begin to think, *"Adultery is normal. Nearly everyone's doing it. Maybe I'm old-fashioned to have sex with my husband/wife only. It would be fun to . . . ."*

> **To avoid adultery:** Decide to obey God, no matter what others do. Spend less time watching TV. Spend more time *studying your Bible...working for God... helping people.* When TV shows adultery, switch it off and give red hot love to *your* husband/wife!

5) Female Dress. Men say, "In church I try to keep my mind on worship, but I notice ladies in tight, short clothes. Then I'm tempted to think evil thoughts."

God says: Men must not think of adultery. (Matt. 5 28) And ladies must be careful how they dress. (1 Pet. 3 3-4)

AVOID SHORT | AVOID TIGHT

To avoid <u>thinking</u> of adultery: *Man,* each time an evil thought enters your mind, make the effort to think something else instead.
Lady, be careful to avoid clothes that give men evil thoughts.
Parent, control the clothes your daughters wear.

Simon: While at university I had intimate relations with 3 girls. I didn't really love any of them. Then I found your book, *"Love & Marriage."* After reading it, I confessed my sins and accepted Christ.

Now I have a wonderful wife and two children.

My problem began last year when my cousin said to me, "Let's go check e-mails at the Internet Cafe." There he showed me how he uses computer-internet to see naked women.

After that I began using my computer at home to do the same thing (whenever my wife wasn't at home). I told myself, "This is not a sin. It's not like the sins I did with university girls. I look at these pictures by *myself.* I'm not hurting anyone."

Yet it was a horrible habit. And it kept growing worse.

Then, today my wife told me that she discovered on my computer that I had looked at the bodies of other women.

I was surprised that she knew enough about computers to discover that.

When I talked with her, my heart broke as I saw her tears.

I *never* want to use my computer like that again. Please help me. I know I will be tempted to do it again.

Dear Simon,

Yes, you will be tempted again. Our advice is: Start a 'group-of-three.' How? Find two other men who believe in Christ. Meet with them once a week. In your first meeting each of you can mention a bad habit that you want to stop. One man may say, "Now that I'm a Christian, I want to stop drinking." Another may say, "I want to stop flirting with girls at work." And you can say, "I want to stop looking at pornography."

Promise each other, "Everything we tell each other will be kept a secret between us three. We will never tell any other person."

Then, each week as you meet, ask each other, "How did you do this week?" Give honest answers. Pray together. Encourage each other. Study the Bible together.

Help other Christians to start 'groups-of-three.' It's hard to fight habits *alone*. Fight habits *together*.

Carry each other's load. (Gal. 6 [2])
Pray for one another. (James 5 [16])
Build up each other. (1 Thes. 5 [11])

Rachel: My husband works in a town so far away that he can come home only once a month. Now he wants me to stay with him there. The problem is: I have a good job right here. I don't know what kind of job I could find there.

Of course, when men are far from their wives, they feel tempted to sin with girls. But my husband is a Christian. Can't Christian men say 'no' to temptations?

Dear Rachel,

They can. But since adultery is a strong temptation, a husband and wife should be careful to satisfy each other sexually. That means they should avoid being separated for a long time.

> Do not stop satisfying each other's sexual needs.
> If both of you **agree** not to have sex for a **brief time**
> so you can pray more, when the brief time is over,
> continue satisfying each other's sexual needs.
> Otherwise Satan may tempt you to do adultery.
> (1 Corinth. 7 ^{5})

We suggest, Rachel, that you say to God, "Lord, because the Bible tells wives and husbands to satisfy each other's needs, I'm going to stay with my husband. Please help me to find a job there (if it's your will). But if it's not your will that I find a job...okay...I will spend more time with our children, and more time working with other believers to spread the gospel. I know you will show my husband and me how to live on the money he earns. Lord, in our marriage we don't want adultery. And we don't want to love money."

God will judge those who commit adultery. Stay away from the love of money.
(Hebrews 13 $^{4-5}$)

ADULTERY   LOVE OF MONEY

Julia: It was a horrible day when I found my husband in bed with a girl. I never thought he would do such a thing. Later he told me, "I still love you, but I also love that girl."

I could not stop crying! I was angry at him, and at her.

Then, somehow I began to blame myself. "This is **my** fault," I told myself. "I've been a terrible wife. I've not been sexy enough, and I haven't been treating him nicely."

So I changed. I did everything I could to make him happy.

Yet he continued his affair with the girl.

Then I asked a church elder for advice. He said, "Stop thinking it's your fault. Let your husband know that he must choose either you or the girl. And don't beg him to choose you. A man looks down on any woman who begs for love."

I was afraid to make my husband choose. I feared he would pick the girl.

Yet I wrote him the following letter.

During the years of our marriage, I have loved you and I still love you now. At our wedding you promised to be faithful to me until death. But now you say that you love me and her. I must say: I cannot be just one of your lovers. You and I are married. We must be faithful to each other as we promised, or we must separate.

I confess; I've not been a perfect wife. I want to improve. But one thing I've done is this: I've had sex with no one but you. It won't work for you to sleep with me and her. That's not marriage.

If you choose her, I will feel heartsick. Yet I know that I can't force you to be faithful. If you choose her, I will need to leave you. Then my life won't be easy, but I will trust God to help me.

I won't judge you, but please remember: God will judge you for each choice you make on earth. (Gal. 6 7-9)

My husband chose to leave the girl. He said my letter opened his eyes.

It was hard for me to forgive him, but I did it.

He didn't like to accept discipline from our church, but he accepted it.

Now our marriage is good again.

As I look back I wonder: When my husband chose adultery, why did I think it was *my* fault? Is it common for a wife to blame herself for the sin of her husband?

89

Dear Julia,

Yes, it's very common. When a husband has sex with another lady, usually his wife tells herself, "It's my fault. If I were a good wife, he wouldn't look at any other lady."

And when a wife commits adultery, the husband usually thinks, "Something's wrong with *me*."

The truth is: Whoever has sex outside marriage, he/she is the one who is guilty—not the partner. (Ezek. 18 20-32)

Julia, you did well to ask your husband to choose either you or the girl.

Of course, he could have decided, "I choose the girl; my wife must leave." Some men do that. But we still say: You were right to make him choose. Even if he had told you to leave, that would have been better than week after week of him sleeping with you and with her.

Aaron: My wife often has sex with other men. Last year I paid a 'prophet'...he used power from *'spirits of departed relatives'* to make her love *only me.* But it didn't work. She still goes to other men.

Recently my brother became a Believer. He witnessed to me, and I accepted Christ. As he and I read the Bible, we are surprised to find verses that say: Never go to any 'prophet' who tries to talk to dead people. (Isaiah 8 19, Lev. 19 31)

So, how can I help my wife to be faithful?

I've told her about Christ. She says, "I am a Christian." But her actions don't show it.

Dear Aaron,

You are wise to study the Bible, and to realise that any 'prophet' who 'talks with the dead' is not a prophet of God. (See also Deut. 18 11-12.) In the Bible, no prophet of God ever said, "I can make someone love you." Anyone who talks like that is a false prophet. (Matt. 24 24)

Here are three ways to help your wife.

1) Request help from your church. Ask your church leaders to choose two Christian ladies who can meet with your wife each week for

prayer and Bible study. We hope she will decide to believe in Christ and live for him. (Gal. 6¹)

2) **Love her unselfishly.** Be kind to her. Notice the things she does well, and tell her how you appreciate her good qualities.

Encourage her to talk about her feelings. Be her friend. (Eph. 5²⁸⁻³³)

3) **Help her by forcing her to choose.** In a kind way, tell your wife that she must be faithful, or she must leave you. Adultery and marriage don't mix. If she chooses to continue in adultery, it means she doesn't want marriage, and so she should go back to the home of her parents. But we pray she will choose to be your faithful wife. (Heb. 13⁴)

Andy: Is it still possible for young people to remain virgins until marriage — in this modern world?

Dear Andy,

Yes. Temptations today are strong, but every Christian has power to say 'no.'

God's grace teaches people of all nations to say 'no' to evil desires, and to live self-controlled, pure lives. (Titus 2¹¹⁻¹²)

Many young people in countries all over the world are living "self-controlled, pure lives."

In our family, both Carol and I were virgins on our wedding day. Each of our children were virgins on their wedding day, and they married virgins—"in this modern world."

Sharon: When I was a young girl, I asked my mother where babies come from. She didn't want to discuss it. So, I asked my friends. They told me many things about sex. Now I realise that everything they told me was wrong or twisted.

I'm now age 25. Today my grandmother told me that when she was young, mothers told daughters:

1) Why menstruation begins.

2) That pregnancy comes from sex.

3) Why a girl must remain a virgin until the day she marries.

And in those days, men told boys:

1) Why they must not make a girl pregnant before marriage.

2) Why a man must care for his wife, children and relatives.

3) How men and women are punished if they do adultery.

This education was given in a natural way; by answering questions, and by telling sad stories or happy stories.

Today some parents tell their kids nothing about sex. So, isn't it good for schools to teach 'sex-education'?

Dear Sharon,

School is not the best place to learn about sex. The best place is at home.

With God's help, we parents must do our best to fill our homes with joyful love. Then let's tell our kids where babies come from. Our words must be true...simple...brief.

Perhaps children who don't have good homes need to learn about sex at school. But Sharon, if you decide to marry, do this:

Marry a man who really loves Christ. In your marriage, love each other and love your kids. This will help them to feel safe and happy. Then, don't assume that schools will do a good job of telling your kids about sex. Instead, you and your husband should tell your own kids about God's good plan for marriage, sex, and babies.

Seth and Hannah: Should we wait until our kids are age 16 to tell them about sex?

Dear Seth and Hannah,

Don't wait that long. Tell each one of them the basic facts of sex before he/she reaches the age of puberty.

Puberty usually begins between ages 10 and 14 for girls, and between 12 and 15 for boys.

Do not tell kids the *details* of sex. They can learn that <u>one</u> <u>week</u> before they marry (by reading this book).

Do this: Before your daughter is age 10, tell her about menstruation. And before your son is age 12, tell him, "Your body will begin to produce sperm. At times the sperm will come out of your penis—as you sleep or when you are awake. Don't worry about that. It's not a sin."

Also tell your son and daughter about:

* *Marriage...sex...pregnancy.* (Be simple and brief.)

* *Sexual desires.* Listen my son (daughter), in the years ahead you will begin to feel *strong* sex-desires. You must control yourself. Say 'no' to sex until your wedding day. Sex means: penis in vagina. Sex is for marriage. Not before.
(2 Tim. 2 22)

* *Joy* comes to people who remain virgins until marriage. *Sorrow* comes to those who do the sin of sex outside marriage. (2 Corinth. 5 10)

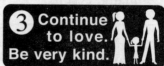

Rhoda: At age 14 I began playing sex with boys. I told myself, "If the boy wears a condom, it's not a sin."

In school our teacher told us, "Long ago people believed that a girl must remain a virgin until marriage, but in the modern world, that has changed."

To me, sex-with-condom was a fun game that modern girls play with boys. (My parents didn't know what I was doing.)

When I reached age 15, Mother told me that we Christians obey our Lord by never having sex until marriage. And she gave me reasons why it's good to wait for marriage.

I was amazed when she said, "The word 'sex' means, *'Penis enters vagina.'* So, sex-with-condom is still sex."

Now I realise I've sinned many times.

Why don't parents tell us about sex before it's too late?

Rhoda's letter reminds all parents, "Tell your children about sex *before it's too late."* Age 15 is too late!

Joshua: During my teenage years, I backslid. I turned my back on my Lord, and wasted my days in sex-for-fun. Two girls got pregnant. The first one wanted to be pregnant — she hoped I would marry her. The other was just an accident.

At age thirty I came back to God.

Then I met a Christian girl whom I wanted to marry. I told her about my past sins, and I promised, "I will never go back to sexual sin."

She said, "God has forgiven you. I forgive you too."

A clinic test showed I had no HIV or other sex-disease.

Then we married. I hoped we'd be happy. But one day she asked me, "How beautiful were those other girls you took to bed? Did you like their bodies more than my body?"

We argued and shouted at each other for an hour.

In the end she promised, "Okay, I forgive you for your sins with those girls. I will never bring up your past again."

I was so happy for that promise; I wrote it in my diary.

But since then we've had more arguments, and she always mentions those girls.

Why can't she forgive and forget?

Dear Joshua,

Your wife feels unhappy that you had sex with someone else. God created humans to feel that way.

Humans are not like animals. Any human will feel hurt if his/her marriage partner has had sex outside marriage.

In the Bible we find a wife saying to her husband:

> Seal me in your heart [have sex with me only],
>   because jealousy burns like fire. (Song of Songs 8 ⁶)

Yes, jealousy burns like fire. Burns take *time* to heal. So it will take time for your wife's jealousy to go away.

Joshua, you and your wife can help your children. How? Do this:

- *Encourage your children to accept Jesus before age 12.*

- *Teach them to remain virgins until marriage.*

- *Warn them that, "Sex before marriage brings jealousy problems in marriage."*

- *Tell them, "Don't backslide. Backsliding will bring long-lasting problems to your life and marriage."*

Backsliding will bring extra trouble to your life, and to your marriage.

BACKSLIDING

GOD'S WAY

God's way isn't easy, but he makes our marriages and homes better, and he gives us eternal life.

No one can make a fool of God. You will harvest what you plant. If you plant sin, you will harvest rot and decay. (Gal. 6 ⁷⁻⁸)

We will not join those who turn back. (Hebrews 10 ³⁹) Even when I walk through the valley, the Lord is with me, and I will live in the house of the Lord forever. (Psalm 23)

Lydia: In my first year of marriage, I never had an orgasm. During loveplay I always asked myself, "Why doesn't my husband know how to make me hot so I can feel orgasm?"

After sex he always went to sleep, and I would cry quietly, feeling sorry for myself because I didn't get satisfied.

Finally I decided to change. Before entry, I asked him to fondle my vagina. Then I put his fingers on my clitoris, and I told him how *excited* he was making me, and what a great *man* he is.

Now he succeeds in exciting me before entry, and after entry I have *marvellous* orgasms.

I'm glad I showed him what I like. He's glad too. He has the feeling, "Just look how I can satisfy my wife!"

Happy are the husbands and wives who talk during loveplay and sex. Oh the joy of showing each other how to excite, how to satisfy!

Victor: What positions are used in sex? Should my wife and I learn the positions by watching a sex-video?

Dear Victor,

There are many positions. Each has its own advantage. The *'male on top'* position has the advantage that: The man can control the action, and this helps him to avoid ejaculating too soon.

The *'female on top'* position has the advantage that: The wife can build her excitement by moving in whatever ways feel most exciting to her.

The advantage of *'both on their side'* is: The penis rubs on the *sides* of the vagina. Some women enjoy that.

Don't watch a sex-video. Don't look at a naked man and woman.

Instead, as husband and wife, tell each other, *"Let's see how many positions we can enjoy."*

Then the two of you can continue using whatever positions both of you enjoy.

Yes, marriage is such a pleasure.

Luke: I'm single and I fear to marry. Why? Because my penis is small. Even when it's hard, it's only 9 cm long.

Some girls say they want to marry a man with a big one. According to them, such men give more pleasure.

How true is that?

Dear Luke,

It's **not** true. A man with a big penis cannot give his wife more pleasure than a man with a small one.

A woman has two 'erotic' [pleasure-feeling] areas:

      a) her clitoris,
      b) the first 5 cm of her vagina.

Notice: Only 5 cm of the vagina are erotic. So, a man does not need a long penis. Just 5 cm are enough. Therefore, Luke, your penis is big enough.

Often a man tells us, "My wife doesn't like sex; I think my penis is too small." Then his wife tells us, *"The problem is: All day he scolds me like a child ... he never talks with me as a friend ... that's why I don't like sex."*

Luke, when you marry, love your wife. Treat her as your friend/partner. And never worry about the size of your penis.

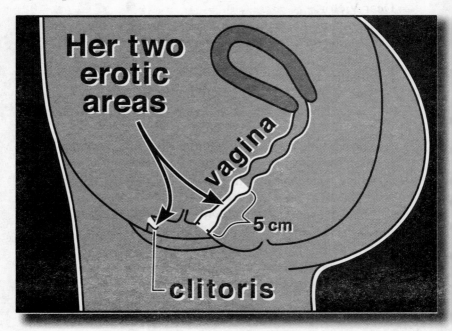

Samuel: I like to enter my wife's vagina from the rear; so that her lovely buttocks press on my stomach. But in rear-entry she fails to reach orgasm. Yet in front-entry she gets orgasms. Why?

Dear Samuel,

The key to orgasm is her 'clitoris.'

In front-entry as your penis moves in her vagina, your penis also rubs her clitoris. That gives her an orgasm.

In rear-entry your penis doesn't touch her clitoris...so she may not reach orgasm.

Samuel, there is a way for you to help your wife to reach orgasm during rear-entry. How? Enter her vagina from the rear...*and fondle her clitoris with your fingers.*

As you move your penis in-and-out, _and_ you continue fondling her clitoris with your fingers for some minutes, probably she will reach orgasm.

Martha: Which positions should we use while I'm pregnant?

Dear Martha,

Here are two suggestions:

a) Rear-entry: The husband and wife lay on their sides with her buttocks against his stomach; then he enters her vagina. This is a good position during pregnancy because he doesn't press on her stomach. The only problem is: In rear-entry, his penis doesn't touch her clitoris. Therefore, while his penis is moving in her vagina, he should continually fondle her clitoris with his fingers . . . until she reaches the joy of orgasm.

b) Sitting: He sits on a chair and she sits with one of her legs on each side of his body. In this position, the penis does not enter her vagina deeply...so it's a good position to use in the 8th month. [See page 164.]

In fact, you may try any position you wish during

pregnancy. And don't worry—if you feel no pain, that means you are not hurting your baby.

Listen, Martha. During pregnancy show love to your husband. Have sex often. Make sex *exciting* for him, and for you. Then your love will grow. And then your baby will be born into a home where the mother and father love each other. Every baby needs exactly that—*a home where his mother and father love each other.*

Joel: I'm not a Christian. Even without Christ and without church, my marriage is okay. Must I accept Christ?

Dear Joel,

Jesus never said, "Come to me if your marriage is bad." He said, "Come . . . I'm the only one who can take you to heaven." (See John 3 [13-18] and 6 [40].)

Perhaps you think, "God will not send me to hell—I'm a nice guy."

The truth is: No one is nice. We all are sinful. Yes, you have sinned, and you cannot enter heaven with your sins. But here is Good News:

God so loved you, Joel, that he sent his only Son to die for your sins. Now, if you choose to accept Christ, he will save you from hell, and take you to heaven. (John 3 [16])

Mark and Ruth: At our Couples-for-Christ meeting you said, "Each husband should know what turns-on a female, and each wife should know what turns-on a male."
What does that mean?

Dear Mark and Ruth,

It means: A husband and wife should understand how different males are from females.

Ruth, you need to understand that males get turned-on by what they *see*. When a man sees a shapely woman in tight clothes, suddenly he is turned-on . . . his body wants sex . . . even if he knows nothing about her personality. Just seeing the shape of her body...that's enough...he feels sexy. Then he must use all his self-control to say 'no' to that temptation and remain faithful to his wife.

Listen, Mark. Females are different. A female gets turned-on when a man satisfies her *emotional* needs. When she sees a nice-looking male body, that doesn't tempt her much. But she begins to feel sexy (turned-on) when she meets a man who talks with her...listens to her, appreciates her ideas...and cares about her feelings. If a guy like that says, "I love you...leave your husband...visit me tonight," she must use all her self-control to say 'no.'

Problems in the Bedroom

In many homes there are bedroom-problems just because the husband and wife don't understand the difference between males and females. For example, a wife enters the bedroom wearing a shapeless nightie. He wishes she would wear a sexy nightie...or nothing! He wants to *see* her. So, he feels disappointed.

She's thinking, "He has seen my body a thousand times...why would he want to see it again?"

The next day when he arrives home from work, he sits and watches TV. He feels tired. He doesn't

want his wife or kids to bother him. At dinner he says less than ten words. He doesn't hate his wife—he just selfishly wants to relax and think of his own needs—not hers.

Then at bedtime she comes out of the bathroom with her nightie sticking to each curve of her body. He wants to touch her *everywhere!*

But she is thinking, "Does he love me? I doubt it. He doesn't talk with me or help me. He only likes to *use my body.*"

She let's him use her, but she doesn't feel loved—she feels used.

How does he feel? He is worrying, "Why doesn't she enjoy sex? Is my penis too small?"

We tell him, "Your penis is okay. Your communication is too small. Talk with your wife. Be a friend to her. Show her that you care about her as a person, not just as a body. Help her care for the kids. Then she will feel loved, and she will feel sexy."

And we tell *her,* "When you are in public, wear clothes that will not turn-on men. But in your bedroom, wear something sexy...just for your husband. That will tell him, *'I love you. I show my body to you—not to other men—just to you!'* "

● Females are turned-on by a man who,
a) "communicates with me as a friend," and
b) "unselfishly cares for me."

● Males are turned-on by seeing the shape of her body.

Listen men: Don't look lustfully at women.

Listen parents: Tell your daughters, "No, you can't wear that. Wear skirts that are not tight and not short. Don't tempt men. Listen to us. We love you." (Matt. 5 ^{28})

Miriam: During sex, our bed squeaks loudly. People can hear us. My husband doesn't care if they hear, but it bothers me.

Dear Miriam,

Just say to your husband, "We women are different from men. As a woman, I would feel more sexy if we had a *quiet* bed."

He will quickly repair the bed, or buy a new one!

Theo: I've been married one year. My problem is: I ejaculate too quickly. During loveplay I always tell my wife not to fondle my penis. But as I start to enter her, when my penis touches her vagina, I ejaculate immediately.

Dear Theo,

It's a mistake to tell your wife, "Don't fondle my penis." Let her fondle you. In fact, here's the best way to do sex:

During loveplay, as you fondle her, she fondles your penis. Soon you will reach the point where you tell her, "Wait . . . I'm close to ejaculating, but I don't want to ejaculate until I'm inside you. So stop fondling me for a few minutes. I need to cool."

During those minutes you continue to fondle her, but she lets your penis cool, until you say, "Okay, fondle me again," and soon after that you will tell her, "Wait . . . I need to cool again."

Repeat that 'fondle-cool . . . fondle-cool' many times.

> *Before you enter her, she fondles your penis, but she doesn't make you ejaculate. Then you enter her. Because she fondled you before entry, you will not ejaculate too soon after entry.*

Don't worry if you have little success the first time you try 'fondle-cool.' It may take weeks. Just remember: Before you enter your wife, let her fondle your penis for a long time — but without making you ejaculate. After some weeks you will find that this is helping you to 'slow down' after entry.

In fact, you will be saying, "Now I succeed in entering without ejaculating . . . then I wait a minute . . . then I start moving in-and-out, and my wife has time to reach orgasm before I ejaculate. It's great!"

Don't buy slow-down medicines. 'Fondle-cool' works better than any medicine. And 'fondle-cool' is enjoyable. It builds love between husband and wife.

Before entry let her fondle you, without making you ejaculate. That will help you not to ejaculate too soon after entry.

Aaron: Does drinking alcohol (beer) help a man/woman to enjoy sex more?

Dear Aaron,

No. A man who has alcohol in his body ejaculates before he wants to.

In a woman, alcohol makes it difficult for her to get excited and reach orgasm.

> Men and women who drink enjoy sex less.

Rebekah: I'm so busy. Every afternoon when I arrive home from work, I cook and care for the children. When I finally get to bed, I'm too tired for sex. I tell myself, "I should satisfy my husband," but usually I just fall asleep. Now my husband complains that I'm not sexy. What can I do?

Dear Rebekah,

Find better times for sex, e.g. Saturday afternoon.

Also, some days tell yourself, "This evening I will give time to my marriage. Instead of cleaning the house, I will invite my husband to our bedroom, *and make it a night he will never forget!"*

Can you ignore the cleaning *every* day. No. But you should ignore it sometimes. Why? Because it's good for marriage to have exciting sex.

Listen Every Husband. Each day when you arrive home, don't just sit. Help your wife. Repair the broken table. Tell a Bible story to the kids. Bathe them. Be like Jesus…He washed men's feet!

> Help your wife. She is physically weaker. (1 Peter 3[7])

Perhaps your culture says, "A *man* should never cook, or care for children." But God says, "A woman is physically weaker, and so a husband should help his wife. If he doesn't help her, his prayers will have less power." (See 1 Peter 3[7].)

Yes, help your wife. Your prayers will have more power. And your bedroom will become more exciting since your wife will not be tired.

Gloria: My husband is *over-sexed!* Every day he wants it. I like sex, but not much. Why? Because I feel unloved. My husband is never interested in conversation with me. I need him to be my friend. But he thinks marriage means sex.

Dear Gloria,

There are different kinds of love.

From your letter, we see that your husband is a person who needs *'sexual love.'* And you need *'emotional love.'*

So your marriage is like this:

My husband doesn't love me. I do well at loving him. I show concern for him as my friend. And I communicate with him. I wish he would love me like that.

My wife doesn't love me. I do well at loving her. I give her sex any time she wants it. I wish she would love me like that.

Your husband assumes that you need the same kind of love that he needs . . . 'sexual love.'

He doesn't know what you really need.

Gloria, sit down with your husband and talk with him like this.

a) Respectfully explain to him that you need *'emotional love.'* Let him know that sex alone is not enough to make you feel loved; but you would feel loved if he would talk with you as his friend, and show interest in you as a person.

b) Tell him, "I now understand that *sex* makes you feel loved. Starting today I will do better at loving you with sex."

After that conversation, hopefully your husband will do better at giving you the kind of love you need.

But don't expect him to be perfect. Sometimes, Gloria, you may think, "Let me leave my husband and look for a man who can satisfy my need for emotional love."

The truth is: No man on earth can satisfy all the needs of your heart.

Jesus can. When he met a woman who had 5 husbands, he told her, "If you continue drinking that water, you will thirst again. Drink the water I give. Then you will be satisfied, and you will have eternal life." (See John 4 [13-14].)

Husband: Be careful to notice the kind of love your wife needs. Does she need you to listen to her problems...or to spend more time with the children...or what? Then love her in <u>that</u> way. (Col. 3 [19])

One wife told us, "I said to my husband, 'Chapter 1 of *Answers for your Marriage* turned on my desire for sex.' He immediately read that chapter! Then our communication improved, and so did our sex."

Isaiah: A nurse told me about a man who needed to have part of his penis removed by surgery. How can I avoid that?

Dear Isaiah,

Wash your penis daily. How? Pull the skin back and wash the head of the penis with warm water and soap. Every man and boy should do that *every day*.

Joe: What kind of lubricant should I put on my penis before entry?...Vaseline, butter, or what?

Dear Joe,

Improve your loveplay. During loveplay ask her, "How can I help you to grow excited? Tell me. Show me."

After 30 minutes of exciting loveplay, probably her

vagina will be wet with 'natural lubrication.' Then you will not need to use any lubricant.

But it is a fact that: Some women produce *little* 'natural lubrication' . . . other women produce *much.* If your wife produces little, then you should use some lubricant.

Don't use Vaseline or butter. Why? They don't wash off with water.

Use "water soluble lubricating jelly" (from a chemist) or "body lotion."

If you use "body lotion," choose one that is *cheap.* Expensive lotions are not good—they contain perfume that is painful to sex organs.

Abigail: I've been married 20 years. When I was a young wife, I desired sex every day. In those years my husband didn't desire it that often, but he's a dear man and he always gave me whatever I wanted.

Now things have changed. For me, one orgasm a month is enough. But my husband wants it every day.

I've discovered how to keep him happy. Nearly every morning I lay on m y side with my back to him; then he enters my vagina from the rear. Usually I feel no need for an orgasm; so I just lay quietly while he enjoys loving me.

And sometimes in the bed, bath or shower, I use my hand to satisfy him. He likes that. So I do it often.

I'm glad to satisfy him. As 1 Corinthians 7 [3] says, "The husband satisfies his wife, and she satisfies him."

Dear Abigail,

Yes, in marriage we joyfully satisfy each other.

Samuel: My wife is a nice person and a true friend to me. She is also sexy. I mean, when we have sex, it's fabulous. The problem is: She doesn't want sex often.

After sex, her body feels satisfied for two weeks, but mine is satisfied for only one day.

What can I do? Many days I feel hungry for sex, and my hunger is not satisfied.

Dear Samuel,

Have a good talk with your wife about your need for more sex. Suggest some ways that she could satisfy you.

Never tell yourself, "If I do adultery, it will be my wife's fault, and so God will not judge me."

The fact is: God will judge you. (Ezekiel 18 [20])

Samuel, even when you don't feel satisfied, say 'no' to adultery. Be a good father to your kids and a good husband to your wife. Enjoy serving Christ together.

> **Wives:** On days when you feel no need for sex, ask your husband how he feels. Then satisfy him in any ways that both of you like.

Abel: I'm age 26. My girlfriend is a strong Christian. I'm also a Christian. I want to have sex with her now. She says, "We must wait until the day of our wedding."

I can't wait. I want to force her to have sex with me, at least once.

Dear Abel,

This is Carol writing. Abel, I must say, "You need to become a Christian."

I realise you claim to be a Christian, but I doubt if you have ever reached the point of saying to Jesus, *"I'm sinful. I believe that you suffered for my sins. Today I take you as my Saviour/Lord. Since you are my Saviour, I will go to heaven when I die. Since you are my Lord, my life will change. I will not live in sin."*

Abel my son, on the day you sincerely talk to Jesus like that, *you will become a Christian.* Then, as you study the Bible, you will see: Sex is for marriage. Not before. And sex must never be forced (rape). [2 Sam. 13 [11-33]]

Eunice: My husband and I have four children. We never had any problem with sex — until two years ago. Then it started. His penis remained soft, no matter what I did to him.

The doctor examined him and said, "You don't have any of the diseases that cause impotence. Go home; try again." ·

Still it remained soft. Sometimes he failed to enter me. Other times he entered, but after a short time it came out by itself. So I didn't get satisfied. We argued. He shouted at me saying, "This is your fault. When a man is impotent, it proves that his wife is having sex with some other guy."

Honestly, I love Christ, and so I never have sex with anyone except my husband.

What do you think is the cause of his impotence?

Dear Eunice,

Impotence can be caused by disease—or by worry. Since the doctor says that your husband has no such disease, probably the cause is worry.

Here's how worry can cause impotence.

A man (let's call him Joe) fell into bed one night very tired because of a hard day at work. His wife felt sexy. She began fondling his penis—but it remained soft. Both Joe and his wife were surprised.

Actually, they should not have been surprised. Joe was just too tired. Any man will find that his penis doesn't get hard if he is too tired. But Joe and his wife didn't know that. They believed the lie that says, "A real man is always ready for sex."

The next night Joe asked her for sex—just to see if he could do it. During loveplay, he kept watching his penis, and worrying.

Because of his worry, it didn't get hard.

Joe and his wife could have avoided that problem.

How? On the first night when he failed to get hard, his wife should have said, "Today your work made you tired. It's okay. I know you are a wonderful, sexy man. We will succeed in the days ahead."

The next night during loveplay, Joe should not have been worrying, "Am I hard?" Instead he should have *enjoyed* fondling his wife. Then, with his mind free of worry, he would have become hard . . . no problem.

It's like sleep

A man cannot get hard if he is worrying—just like a man cannot fall asleep if he is worrying.

Picture a man in bed trying to fall asleep, and telling himself, "Tomorrow I have much work to do. I must fall asleep. Am I falling asleep? I must sleep now. *I must!*"

He will never get to sleep like that. To fall asleep, he must stop worrying about sleep, and let his mind think about other things. Then sleep will come automatically.

Similarly, to get hard, a man must stop thinking about 'hard.' He must just enjoy touching his wife. Then he will get hard automatically.

Spend five weeks in 'loveplay-without-worry'

Eunice, here is how you and your husband can stop worrying and get victory. For five weeks enjoy loveplay each night, but don't even try to have sex. That will help your husband to relax, knowing that, "Tonight my wife will not ask me to enter her. We will just enjoy each other."

Have a bath together. Then go to bed. Kiss. Fondle each other's sex organs. Enjoy rubbing each other's body with lotion.

As you and your husband are enjoying loveplay, don't think, "Somehow I must make him hard."

Forget 'hard.'

These five weeks are a time to *enjoy* each other, with no worry about 'hard.'

Your husband will feel glad as he realises, "My wife doesn't look down on me. She won't make jokes about me. I don't need to worry. She loves me. I love her."

As you continue 'loveplay-without-worry' each night for some weeks, sooner or later both of you will be enjoying the loveplay so much that you are not even thinking about 'hard'... and then you will happen to notice: *It's hard!* He will enter you. It will be great!

Will that be the end of his impotence? No, but it will be the beginning of victory.

After that, sometimes he will still find that he can't get hard. When that happens, don't worry—just enjoy loveplay. Perhaps it will take months for the problem to disappear.

Some men take pills to make their penis hard. But 'loveplay-without-worry' works better than pills.

Paul: Can smoking cause impotence? Can alcohol cause it?

Dear Paul,

Smoking: Yes, tobacco smoke partly blocks the arteries. That makes it difficult for a man to get hard.

Men who stop smoking often say, "Now I *enjoy* sex. I wish I had stopped smoking years ago. In fact, I never should have started."

Alcohol: Men who continue drinking for years may reach the point where they find, "Now I never get hard."

Don't smoke or drink.

Tom: Which happens more often, A) or B)?

    A) Sex-problems cause a couple to stop loving each other.

    B) A couple stops being sweet all day long, and that gives them sex-problems at night.

Dear Tom,

'B)' happens more often than 'A).'

If a husband and wife stop being kind during the day, soon their sex will no longer be fun.

Elizabeth: I'm a married woman aged 28. I fail to enjoy sex. I wish I could get excited and feel pleasure, but I never do.

    My husband is a good man. During loveplay he tries to excite me, but then he always feels disappointed when he sees how I don't enjoy it.

Dear Elizabeth,

Read this with your husband. Here are 4 things that will help you to enjoy sex.

    1) Think right. Long before bed-time, start thinking

about the joy of sex with your husband. Then, while you are having sex, don't be thinking, "Tomorrow I must clean the house and...." Instead just think about the intimate joy of touching each other's body.

2) Talk. Elizabeth, during loveplay you are free to say, "Please wet your fingers with lotion and fondle my vagina. That's nice. Now fondle my clitoris...here, let me show you. Not hard. Yes, that's perfect. Please kiss me. Now kiss me here and here."

Why can you talk freely? Because you are *married.* (Mark 10[8])

3) Be active. Don't just lay still. Fondle your husband while he is fondling you. Whenever you feel pleasure, don't be quiet. Let your body move!

4) Start it. Do you wait for your husband to chase you, like a rooster chasing a chicken? Elizabeth, you are a human, not a chicken. Human females have strong desires, just like males do. (1 Corinth. 7[3])

So, when your husband says, "Let's have sex," go for it. On other days, *you* may 'start it' yourself. Yes, you are free to kiss him and say, "Let's have sex tonight—or *now!*" (Song 7[12])

Praise God, my wife loves and desires me!

Audrey: My husband and I want a baby. Can I get pregnant even if I fail to reach orgasm?

Dear Audrey,

Yes, you can get pregnant without an orgasm.

Amos: My wife has never had an orgasm. Yet she enjoys sex.

Dear Amos,

Some women feel unsatisfied if they don't reach orgasm, but other women say, "Even if I don't reach orgasm, I enjoy sex—as my husband holds me in his arms and tells me of his love."

So, Amos, nothing is wrong with your wife. Many women live happy, fulfilled lives without any orgasms.

Abner: Why do so many people get HIV? How can I help them?

Dear Abner,

A certain man (let's call him 'Sam') had sex with a young girl. He told himself, "She is so young; she couldn't have HIV." But six weeks before this, a guy who was HIV+ had sex with her. So the disease went from that guy—to the young girl—to Sam.

For the next few years, Sam didn't know that he was now HIV+. He still felt strong—not sick in any way. So he continued sex with girls, and he told himself, "I will never get HIV," not realising he already had it! Neither did he realise that he was passing HIV to girls.

Then, five years after his sex with the 'young girl,' he began having diarrhoea and fever.

At a clinic a nurse told him that he was HIV+.

Sam felt angry! "Why me? Which girl gave it to me?"

Sam's relatives refused to help him. They called him, "Sexual-sinner."

On top of that, his mind had no peace. He realised, *"Probably I've passed HIV to a dozen girls, and those girls may have passed it to other guys . . . ."*

Sam wanted to die! But he felt afraid to stand before God—his Creator and Judge.

Let's help people

Abner, it's good that you want to help people like Sam. You are like Jesus. He helped people that nobody else would help. (Mark 1 41)

Perhaps you wonder, "If I touch people with HIV, will the disease pass to me?"

The answer is: You will not catch HIV by shaking hands, eating from the same dish, using the same toilet . . . . But you can catch HIV by touching their body-liquids: urine, stool, vomit, pus, milk, blood…or things such as needles, razors, toothbrushes that have blood on them.

A nurse can tell you how to help people who have HIV/AIDS, without catching the disease yourself.

As you are caring for someone with AIDS, tell him/her about Jesus. Perhaps he/she will say, "Jesus is turning his back on me because of my sins." You can reply, "Let me tell you the Bad News and the Good News."

Bad News . . . Good News

The <u>Bad</u> News is: All of us should go to hell because of our sins.

The <u>Good</u> News is: God can forgive us. Why? Because Jesus suffered for the sins we have done. (Rom. 3 23 and Rom. 6 23)

God says, "Believe in my Son, Jesus. Accept him as your Master and Saviour. Then I will make you my child, and I will give you a gift—the gift of eternal life." (John 1 12 and John 3 16)

That's Good News! Let's tell it to everyone—to people who are suffering, and to people who are healthy.

Jacob: I'm at university. How can I avoid HIV?

Dear Jacob,

One thing we must say is: Wear gloves when you touch anyone's body-liquids: vomit, urine, stool, blood….

But HIV spreads more often by *sex* than by those liquids. So, the more important thing we must say is:

Don't have sex with anyone who is HIV+.

The problem is: There is no way you can look at a person and say, "I'm sure this one isn't HIV+."

Therefore, *the best way to avoid HIV is:*

1) **Before marriage:** Do not have sex with anyone.

2) **After marriage:** You and your wife must have sex with each other only.

3) **No homosexual sin:** A man must not have sex with a man. A lady must not have sex with a lady.

It's interesting that *"the best way to avoid HIV"* is: Obey the Bible. Yes, obey the Bible like this:

1) **Before marriage:** 1 Corinth. 6 [18] says, "Run away from sex outside marriage."

2) **After marriage:** Proverbs 5 [18-23] says, "Be happy with your wife. Enjoy the girl you married. She is as beautiful as a deer. Let her breasts delight you. Let her love fill you with pleasure. Why give your love to another lady? God sees everything you do. The sins of a man are a trap.... He dies because he refused to listen."

3) **Homosexual sin:** Lev. 20 [13] says, "If a man has sex with a man, both of them have sinned and should die."

Do not be deceived; people who have sex outside marriage ... and people who do homosexual sins... will not inherit God's Kingdom. In the past, some of you were like that, but now you are washed, and you are living a sanctified, new life. (1 Corinth. 6 [9-11])

HIV isn't the only disease that spreads by sex. There are others, such as syphilis and gonorrhea (drop). We call such diseases: Sexually Transmitted Infections (or STIs). Syphilis and gonorrhea have been on earth for hundreds of years. HIV is a new STI that began about 1980.

Here's a fact of history: In a nation where people do much sex-sin, STIs increase. But when many people have sex in marriage only, STIs decrease.

> **If everyone would have sex in marriage only, HIV would soon disappear.**
> (So would other STIs.)

Today in most nations STIs are increasing.

Medical science is failing to stop the increase. Our only hope is: Return to God's way:

Be wise. Choose to live God's way.

Before marriage say 'no' to sex.
1 Thes. 4 3-5)

Enjoy sex in marriage.
(1 Corinth. 7 3-5)

Refuse to do adultery.
(Heb. 13 4)

Now Jacob, you may be thinking, "Even if I say 'no' to sexual sin, perhaps the girl I marry will be HIV+, and she will pass it to me."

Here are two things you can do about that:

a) **Choose carefully.** When choosing a wife, look for a girl who loves Christ, and says 'no' to guys who want sex before marriage?"

Of course, it's hard to know if she is really a girl who says 'no' and is HIV-. Therefore the next step is: Go for a test at a clinic.

b) **Go for a HIV test.** Before you marry, go to a clinic, ask them to test you for HIV and other STIs. Get a written statement from the clinic, and give it to the girl you plan to marry. Then ask her to do the same.

> **Every church should make this rule:**
> If a man and lady wish to have their wedding in our church, both must show each other a clinic-statement showing his/her HIV status.

Jacob, here is a brief answer to your question.

How to avoid HIV

1. **Before marriage, obey God — say 'no' to sex.**

2. **When looking for a husband/wife, try to find someone who is a virgin. Or, if he/she says, "In the past I lived in sin, but now I've accepted Christ," take many months to see: Is he/she saying 'no' to anyone who wants sex outside marriage?**

   Also, before marriage both of you should go to a clinic to be tested for HIV and other STIs.

3. **After marriage, obey God — no adultery.** *Enjoy sex with your husband/wife. Satisfy him/her.*

4. **Wear gloves when you touch body-liquids. And do no homosexual sin.**

Many people do not follow those four, especially numbers 1 and 3.

For example, Grace is a university student. She has a sex-partner. She hopes to avoid HIV by using condoms. She refuses to have sex with him unless he wears one. Yet the fact is: Condoms may help — but condoms do not keep a person 100% safe from HIV. So Grace is in danger.

Hannah is more careful. When Dan asked her for sex, she put gel (cream) on herself to kill any HIV that he may have. And then she handed him a condom. But she is still in danger because even condom with gel cannot be trusted 100%.

Grace, Hannah and Dan need to turn from their sins and accept Christ. Then the Holy Spirit will give them power to live a *new life*.

Have you, Jacob, ever accepted Christ? Do it today.

> "Whoever believes in the Son has eternal life.
> Whoever rejects the Son, will not enter heaven;
> God's anger will remain on him." (John 3 36)

> If anyone is in Christ, he is a new creation.
> His old life goes away; he begins a *new life*.
> (2 Corinth. 5 17)

Deborah: I don't want my son of age 4 to get HIV. Each time I take him to the clinic, I tell the nurse, "Please use a needle that is sterile."

Am I overly careful?

Dear Deborah,

You are doing well. But don't forget: Most people who have HIV got it from sex—not from a clinic.

Therefore, as your son grows up, be an example to him. Teach him to have faith in Jesus. Pray that when he reaches age 12, he will be able to say,

> "I've accepted Jesus. I'm on my way to heaven.
> I will live his way. I will not have sex with
> anyone until the day I marry."

Beatrice: Last year my husband died of AIDS. Then I got TB. I became so sick that I couldn't get out of bed.

In our church I was chairlady of the 'Gospel to All Nations' committee. Because of TB, I had to resign as chairlady.

Then the doctor informed me that I'm HIV+.

In my entire life I've had sex with my husband only. So I assume I got the disease from him.

Now two women visit me every day. I thank God for them. But I hear that the new chairlady is saying, "Probably Beatrice did adultery...now God is punishing her."

God knows I've done no sexual sin. I just need my friends to stand with me!

Comments on Beatrice's letter:

● If everyone had sex in marriage only, HIV would soon disappear. So HIV is the result of sex-sin.

● But some people get HIV—not from their own sin—but from the sin of others, (e.g. babies, rape-victims, people who get it from blood, stool, vomit…, and people like Beatrice).

● Let's care for *everyone* who has HIV. (Luke 10 [34], Matt. 24 [36])

● Let's tell all people to obey God by having sex in marriage only. If they do that, HIV will decline. (2 Chron. 6 [26-28], 7 [13-14])

Sarah: I realise HIV is spread by sex. What *other* diseases can a person catch from sex?

Dear Sarah,

There are many **S**exually **T**ransmitted **I**nfections **(STIs)**, such as: *Gonorrhea, Herpes, Genital warts, Syphilis….*

Gonorrhea (drop) is a disease that causes yellow liquid to drip from the penis/vagina, and pain in the abdomen, or pain while passing urine. If you ever have those symptoms, go to a clinic *that same day*. Don't wait. If you wait many days, gonorrhea can make you childless.

Herpes is painful sores on the penis or vagina. After two weeks the sores go away. But later they return for another two weeks. Doctors cannot cure herpes. So the sores continue to return now-and-then for the person's whole life.

> You can avoid all STIs. How? The same way you avoid HIV. (See page 115.)

Genital warts are small growths on the penis/vagina. Clinics have helpful medicine. But the warts may cause the bad disease, 'cancer of the uterus.'

> **Condoms fail to prevent some STIs.**

Syphilis causes sores on the penis/vagina. Clinics can cure syphilis. But some people die of this disease—just because they *wait too long* before going to a clinic.

Listen all women: When you are pregnant, go to a clinic to be tested for STIs. Why? Usually doctors can prevent STIs from passing to your baby.

Some signs of STIs are:

● **Lumps, spots, warts or sores on the penis, vagina, or mouth. These may be painful or painless.**

● **Males may notice a yellow liquid 'drop' from the penis. And they may feel pain when passing urine.**

● **Females may notice a yellow liquid from the vagina, or pain in the lower abdomen.**

If you find any of these signs, go to a clinic *immediately*. Don't wait even one day. Many STIs can be cured.

Because of all the STIs on earth today,
we tell every boy and every girl:
● Remain a virgin until your wedding.
● Marry a person who is a virgin.
● Have sex with your husband/wife only.
● Then you will never get any disease from sex.

Anna: My sister lived in sin for three years. Yesterday she repented and came back to Christ.

Then today the clinic told her, "You are HIV+."

I love her so much. What advice can I give her so that she will live as long as possible?

Dear Anna,

Tell your sister: Although you are HIV+, you can remain healthy for a long time. How? Do this:

Take the medicine your doctor prescribes. Get plenty of sleep. Exercise by going for a long walk daily. Never smoke or drink alcohol. Eat good food (eggs, milk, beans, raw vegetables, fruit....)

Avoid worry and anger. (Those make your body weak.)

When you are sick, go to a clinic immediately. If you delay, the sickness will get worse (since HIV weakens your body-defenses).

Don't go back to sexual-sin. Why? Three reasons:

  a) You are single. God commands us to have no sex outside marriage.

  b) If you have sex with a guy, he may pass a STI to you. Your body-defenses are weak; therefore a simple STI could kill you.

  c) You don't want to be responsible for passing HIV to anyone.

Use each of your days on earth wisely. Encourage young people to repent, accept Christ, and serve him.

Daily let these verses build up your soul. Psalm 73 ^{26}, Psalm 94 $^{18\text{-}19}$, John 11 ^{25}, John 14 $^{16\text{-}20}$, Rom. 8 ^{18}, 1 Corinth. 4 $^{14\text{-}16}$, 1 Thes. 4 $^{14\text{-}18}$, 1 Pet. 5 ^{7}, Rev. 21 ^{4}.

Caleb: I heard a preacher say, "The *'sins of youth'* can make a man or a lady childless." How true is that?

Dear Caleb,

It's true. For example, a school-boy named Mark had sex with a girl. She had a STI called 'gonorrhea' or 'drop.' So that disease passed from her to Mark.

But Mark didn't realise he had any disease. Then he had sex with a school-girl named Ruth. So, gonorrhea passed to Ruth.

Five days later, Mark felt pain when urinating. He went to a clinic and was cured.

But Ruth didn't realise she had a disease. Mark *should*

have told her, "I had gonorrhea. So you probably have it now. Go to a clinic."

But he said nothing.

For six weeks Ruth felt no pain. Yet the gonorrhea was quietly destroying her Fallopian tubes.

Then one day she felt pain in her abdomen. She went to a clinic. The doctor told her, "Ruth, you came to me too late. Gonorrhea has already destroyed your Fallopian tubes. You will never be a mother. I'm sorry. Please tell your friends to spend their school-days studying—not playing with sex."

It's sad that so many women worldwide are childless because of gonorrhea.

Gonorrhea can also make a man childless. If a man gets gonorrhea, and he *waits many days* before going to a clinic, the gonorrhea slowly destroys his sperm tubes. After that he can still ejaculate a white liquid that looks normal, but the liquid contains no sperm. So he can never make a woman pregnant.

> STIs remind the people of every nation that it's better to obey our Creator than to live in sex-sin.

Therefore, Caleb, the preacher was correct when he said, *"The 'sins of youth' can make a person childless."*

Of course, not all childlessness is the result of sin. So we must not judge a childless couple by saying, "They must have sinned."

But let's warn young people that sin can cause childlessness, as well as many other sorrows.

Grace: I realise HIV can spread when there is penis in vagina. Can HIV also spread from vagina to mouth? And from penis to mouth?

Dear Grace,

Yes, HIV and other STIs can spread from one person's vagina/penis to another person's mouth.

Lois: My husband and I have been married ten years. We never have sex with anyone else, just with each other.

Sometimes we use our mouths to love each other's sex-organ.

a) Is that sin?

b) Will 'mouth to penis/vagina' give us any disease?

Dear Lois,

a) No, it is not sin. Why? Because you are married. A husband and wife are free to love in any ways they both desire.

b) Will you and your husband give each other a disease by 'mouth to penis/vagina'? No. Why? Because both of you never have sex with others, and so you have no STI.

But, Lois, if you or your husband ever have sex with someone else, you could get a STI from that person, and then you could pass that STI to your husband/wife.

Therefore we say to both of you, *"Continue having sex with each other only. Then you will never get any disease from each other's vagina or penis."*

Disease can spread from the anus. But no disease spreads from penis/vagina except STIs.

Keep yourself pure. (1 Tim. 5 ^{22})

To people who are pure, everything is pure. (Titus 1 ^{15})

Patrick: I'm president of a company. My wife and I have 3 sons.

Two years ago we joined a club for rich people. All the club members liked to meet in a home and have sex with one another's wives/husbands. My wife and I felt it was not wrong since we did it with each other's consent.

Then our neighbour invited us to an Easter service at his church. There we decided to believe in Christ, and we asked him to forgive our many sins.

Now we have stopped committing adultery.

But today our doctor told my wife that she is pregnant. I feel angry. I doubt that I'm the father. She was having more sex with other men than with me. I don't know what to do.

Dear Patrick,

On the day you and your wife chose to accept Christ,

God forgave your sins. Yet, the sins both of you did will have some results in your present life.

One result is: You don't know who made your wife pregnant.

Another result is: For a long time your minds will continue thinking, "My husband/wife was not faithful to me. I wish he/she had always loved me—and only me."

Another result may be: Because of adultery, you may now have sex-diseases such as herpes, syphilis, or HIV.

What can you do?

1) Forgive each other—like Christ forgave you. This may take some time. God will help you.

2) Ask a doctor/nurse to check both of you for sex-diseases.
   [See page 117.]

3) Pray together. Study the Bible together. Begin with the book of John, Colossians 3^{1-19}, and Eph. 4^{17} to 6^{18}.

4) Patrick, accept and love your wife's child the same as you love your own sons.

5) Say to your friends at the club and to everyone, "Sin spoils life, and the day of judgement is coming. Please turn to Christ. He will forgive your sins, give you heaven, and walk with you each day." [See pages 27, 28, 124.]

Andrew: I work in the city. I'm able to go home to my wife and kids only once a month.

Here in this city, may I have a 'girl-for-sex'? Would that be sin?

The custom of our people says, "When a man has sex with a girl, that is not a sin against his wife. But if a wife does adultery, that's a sin against her husband."

Dear Andrew,

That 'custom' is in every country on earth. Yes, all over Europe, Africa, America and Asia, you find that a man gets angry if his wife has a 'lover,' but he thinks that she should not get angry about his 'lady-friend.'

However, God commands **men and women** not to do adultery. (Ex. 20 14, Prov. 5 15)

Andrew, you must choose. Either you will follow God, or the customs of man.

Choose wisely. Remember, after death you will be judged by God—not by man. (Rev. 20 12)

Also, if you have a 'girl-for-sex,' she may have a STI. That STI may pass to you, and from you to your wife.

The best thing you can do is: Accept Christ. And help your wife to accept him. Then pray saying, "Lord, please help my wife and I to find a way to stay together."

While you are looking for an answer to that prayer, every morning promise God, "Today I will be faithful to my wife."

Vincent: I believe a man needs to love girls. Even in the Bible, David did it to Bathsheba.

Two years ago I told a girl, "I love you," but I didn't really love her. I just wanted sex. She fell pregnant. I refused to admit that I was the father. Then she gave birth to a baby who looks exactly like me. I don't want to marry her because I don't like her behaviour. Now she wants me to buy clothes for the child, but I want to complete my education.

Why do I have such trouble?

Dear Vincent,

Good question. *Why do you have such trouble?*

Answer: Life always has trouble, and when you choose to sin, that sin brings you *extra* trouble.

David chose to sin with Bathsheba…and his sin brought him *extra* trouble.

(Study 2 Samuel 12 10, 12 19, 18 33, and Heb. 12 6.)

Then David repented, and he asked God to wash him. (Psa. 51)

Vincent, you should do the same. Choose to become a Christian.

> Life always has trouble. On top of that, sin brings _extra_ trouble.

A PRAYER TO BECOME A CHRISTIAN

Lord, I have sinned. My sins bring me trouble. And I know that my sins should separate me from you forever. Yes, I should go to hell.

Now I believe: Jesus died to save me from hell.

And now I repent. That means; I now change my mind. Instead of wanting to live in sin, I want to live for you. Today I make you my Lord. (Acts 2 ^{38})

Since Jesus died for my sins, I will enter heaven.

Then, Vincent, as a Christian, your first step should be: Provide your child with education, clothes, *and love*.

(1 Tim. 5 ^{8}, Malachi 4 ^{6})

Rachel: I'm a single girl aged 25. I've never had sex. Some people in the office where I work say that I'm "too religious," or "abnormal." Yet, I decided long ago to obey my Lord by waiting for marriage.

I'm a friendly person. I enjoy talking with everyone, male or female. But when a guy tries to convince me to give in, I tell him, "Move off."

I've always told myself, "God has a good husband for me—a man who will be glad that I'm a virgin."

Now it has happened. Luke has asked me to marry him. He's a strong Christian. I'm so excited! I feel like I'm walking on a cloud!

He, too, has been laughed at for remaining a virgin.

Our wedding will be immediately after he completes his training as a medical doctor.

My two sisters try to enjoy sin, yet they always fear HIV. I tell them, "Turn to Jesus. He will save you from hell. And he will empower you to turn from sin."

Next year our church will send Luke and me to the country of Mali so we can help people there and spread the gospel.

I feel afraid to leave home, but Christ will be with us.

Dear Rachel,

We admire your love for Christ. You don't need to fear leaving home and going to Mali. Jesus said:

> "I have all power... Therefore, go...
> make disciples of all nations...
> *I am with you always....*" (Matt. 28 $^{18-20}$)

> "The Holy Spirit will give you *power to witness* here...and to the ends of the earth." (Acts 1 ^{8})

Open your eyes, and you will find people in your nation, and people in other nations (near and far) who need to hear how Christ gives eternal life. Ask your church to pray and send out believers who will go and tell them the Good News.

See page 140

Esther: In two weeks I'm going to marry. Following the custom of our people, last week grandmother inspected my hymen to be sure it's not broken. Now in these days before the wedding, the custom is that I must stretch my hymen with my fingers so that my husband will be able to enter easily.

My problem is: Each time I stretch it, I get an orgasm.

Now I worry. Perhaps God is angry with me for having orgasms before marriage. Maybe I can no longer sing in the church choir.

Dear Esther,

You have not done a sexual sin. If you had allowed a man to put his penis into your vagina, that would be a sin.

In other words, sex before marriage is a sin. But having an orgasm isn't a sin. God is not angry with you. Continue in the choir. [The 'hymen' is explained on pages 61-62.]

After you marry, you and your husband will enjoy serving Christ together in your nation or in other nations.

Sharon: I'm in love with the preacher at church. Every Sunday instead of listening to his sermon, my mind dreams about *him*. I try to push all romantic thoughts out of my mind, but soon they return, stronger than ever.

The problem is: I'm single—he has a wife and two kids.

My love is so strong, I attend Tuesday Bible-Study just to see him. He has never said that he loves me, but I can see in his eyes that he does.

Please don't tell me, "Join a different church."

If I leave this church, everyone will ask *why*.

What can I do? Should I tell him how I feel so that he can give me advice?

Dear Sharon,

No, don't tell him how you feel. A man can be tempted if a lady tells him, "Please advise me. I feel love for *you*."

Do nothing that will tempt him to touch you. Never allow yourself to be alone with him. And stop attending that Tuesday Bible-Study. Join another Bible-Study; one that he doesn't attend.

Then, if your desire for him continues, join a different church…any church that teaches the Bible correctly. Don't say why you are leaving your present church. Just leave. The Bible says, "Run away from sexual-sin." (1 Corinth. 6 [18])

Nathan: Priscilla and I love each other deeply. We plan to marry next year.

I want to obey God by not having sex with her before marriage. But will I succeed??? I'm a person with very strong sex-desires. Before I became a Christian, I had sex with many girls. Then, two years ago, my friend showed me what the Bible says about sin, hell, and Christ. I chose Christ as my Saviour. Since that day I've not had sex. I've been helped by staying with good Christian friends here at the Teacher Training College. Together we study the Bible. Then we tell Bible stories to children, and we witness in homes.

My problem is: After I complete my training, I will be sent to teach in a rural school. If Priscilla visits me there, how will I escape having sex with her? Or, if she doesn't visit me, how will I avoid having sex with ladies in that area?

Please, please help me. I don't want to do sex-sin. I don't want a baby before marriage. And I don't want HIV or any other STI.

Dear Nathan,

You are not the only man who has strong sex-desires. Men everywhere on earth have such desires. Why did God give men and ladies strong desires. Because he wants husbands and wives to enjoy sex in marriage.

God's law is: Control your desires; have sex in marriage only. (Heb. 13⁴)

Satan tempts us, but all over the world there are men and ladies who are winning the victory. Nathan, you can have victory too.

When you arrive in the rural area, look for two Christian men and say to them, "Every week let's meet for prayer and Bible study (the three of us). And each time we meet, let's ask each other hard questions such as: Are you saying 'no' to sex outside marriage?"

Together read this powerful booklet, "The Power of Christ in My Heart."

Refuse to obey Satan. Your brothers all over the world have the same temptations. (1 Peter 5⁹)

Encourage one another. Build up each other. (1 Thes. 5¹¹)

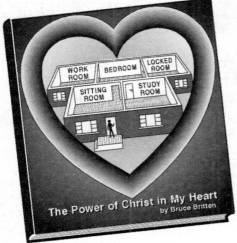

The Power of Christ in My Heart
by Bruce Britten

This booklet helps anyone who needs the power of Christ. Would you like to read it?
Your free copy is on pages 128-136.

The Power of Christ in My Heart
by Bruce Britten*

When I was a very young man, I realised: Christ is knocking on the door of my heart.

"Come in," I said. "I trust you to wash away my sin and give me eternal life. Yes, you may stay in my heart."

When Christ enters a person's heart, he finds many rooms—a study room, sitting room, workroom, bedroom, and perhaps a locked room. He wants to make wonderful improvements in every room.

On the day Christ entered my heart, the first room he

* Based on *My Heart—Christ's Home*, Munger, InterVarsity Press.

went to was my study room. "Let's spend time together in this room every morning," he said. "What joy we can have...studying the Bible together...talking freely with each other!"

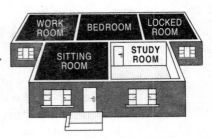

I loved the idea. How exciting, to spend time with Christ every day!

We began to meet early each morning. As we read the Bible together, he showed me where my life must change. And I began to see what great love he has for me. My heart warmed. How I enjoyed those times!

But somehow...as days passed, I began spending less time with Christ. Why? I don't know. I seemed to be busy. It was examination time at the university. After graduating I was busy with my job. Most evenings I worked on a computer course. Sometimes I missed the Bible study time for a whole week.

One morning as I was hurrying out of the house, I noticed the door to the study room was open. Looking in, I saw Christ sitting there...alone. Suddenly I realised: He is my guest—I invited him into my heart—but I spend so little time with him.

"Master, I'm sorry," I said as I entered the room. "Have you been *waiting here...for me...every morning?*"

"Yes," he said sadly. "Each day I feel excited as I come here. I know that you can become a powerful Christian as you study the Bible with me. And I know how your prayers can work to spread the gospel to all nations."

That day I realised: *Nothing is more important than daily Bible study and prayer.*

All Scripture is breathed by God. Teach all of it to people. It will correct their errors. It will train them to live right. (2 Tim. 3^{16})

Bedroom

One morning as Christ and I were in the study room, he looked at me with love and said, "Your heart has other rooms. If you invite me, I will enter each room. I will bring light and joy to every room."

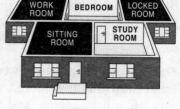

"I invite you right now!" I said warmly. "Let's go."

He walked straight to my bedroom.

There he looked at me and said, "I understand how you feel. As a young man, your body feels sexual desires. Those desires are *strong.* Female bodies attract you. Sometimes you doubt that you can succeed in remaining a virgin until marriage. Satan tells you, 'It's un-natural and impossible to keep sex for marriage only.'"

I felt amazed that Christ understood my temptations.

"Remember this," Christ said. "With my power any young person—male or female—can succeed in keeping sex for marriage only. I can forgive my people if they fall into a sin, but any fall always brings sorrow to their lives, and to me. Therefore I tell you: *Run away from sin.* And I promise: Each time you are tempted, I will make a way for you to escape."

With Christ in my heart, I've succeeded in completely avoiding the sin of sex outside marriage.

All praise goes to him—not to me. He always provides a way to escape.

> Your temptations are no greater than the ones other humans have. God is faithful. Whenever a temptation comes to you, he will provide a way for you to escape.
> (1 Corinth. 10 [13])

Fun

On Saturday morning Christ asked me, "As a young person, where do you go when you want to have fun?"

Silently I looked down at the floor. I didn't want him to know.

That evening as I was leaving the house, he said, "I see you are going out. Good. I want to go with you."

"*Wait*," I said. "You shouldn't go where I'm going now. Tomorrow we can go together . . . to a prayer meeting. But now I'm going . . . ah . . . somewhere."

"I'm sorry," he said with love in his eyes. "When I entered your heart, I hoped we would be friends, and do *everything* together."

As I walked out of the house, I just said, "Okay . . . tomorrow."

As I spent that evening with my friends, I didn't do anything bad, yet I knew: Christ would not enjoy this.

When I arrived back home, I went straight to him. "Lord," I said, "I'm sorry. From now on, let's do everything together."

Smiling, Christ said, "Don't think that I want to spoil your fun. I'm going to make your life better—not worse. You will be surprised when you see how enjoyable life can be."

Then Christ and I went together to a 'Youth-Weekend-of-Bible-Teaching.' There I became friends with three young men who loved to serve God.

> **Christ fills life with joy and purpose.**

After that, whenever I met my non-Christian friends, I told them about Christ. At first no one listened, but eventually two of them repented and joined the church.

What joy we Christian young people had in choir, Bible-study, discussions, picnics, and fun activities!

How we loved to evangelise in schools! What unity we

felt as we spent days together starting a church in a new area!

> Christ said, "I came to give real life,
> joyful, overflowing life!" (John 10 [10])

Sitting Room

"May I enter your sitting room?" Christ asked politely.

"Of course," I said. "Let's watch TV together."

As Christ entered my sitting room, his eyes noticed the magazines on the shelf. Then he sat down with me to watch TV.

Suddenly, I felt embarrassed.

Until then, I'd never felt guilty about my magazines, or the TV programmes I watched. But now that Christ was in this room, I was ashamed.

Quickly I switched off the TV and said, "Master, this room needs big changes. Will you help me?"

"Yes," he said, "we will find better magazines. And tell me, are those the best TV programmes you can find?"

"I've tried to find up-lifting programmes," I replied honestly, "but I can't find many."

"You don't need *many*," Christ said with a smile. "In fact, you've been spending too much time watching TV. Please show me what you are producing in your workroom."

Workroom

As Christ entered my workroom, he noticed that the tools had not been used for a long time. Dust covered everything. I'd been thinking: I can't do much work because I don't

have good tools like other people have.

Christ looked around and said, "This room has excellent tools. What are you producing?"

I showed him three half-finished projects:

'Witnessing to Relatives,' 'Preaching in Prisons,'
and 'Teaching Sunday School.'

"Lord," I said weakly, "I'm sorry I stopped working on those. The reason is...my tools are not great. Other people have great ability and talents—but not me."

"Do you want to do better?" he asked.

"*Yes!*" I replied excitedly.

Then Christ and I began working together. How I love working with him!

Now, when I preach or teach Sunday School, I trust *his* power...and he changes lives!

And when I get on a bus, I silently pray, "Lord, help me to explain the Good News clearly to the person sitting next to me."

Later as I'm getting off the bus, sometimes the person says, "Thanks for showing me how to be a Christian. This is the best day of my life."

Then I'm reminded: *The power of Christ works...even through a no-ability guy like me.* (Acts 4^{13})

Never again will I say, "I can't do much because I don't have great talents."

Christ said, "I have all power.
Therefore, go...
Make disciples. Teach them.
I am with you always." (Matthew 28$^{18\text{-}20}$)

Locked Room

One day when I arrived home, Christ told me, "There's a bad smell in the house . . . something is rotten. The smell is coming from that locked room."

I knew exactly what he meant. In my house there was one room I always locked. There I kept secret bitterness against two people I hated.

I followed Christ as he walked straight to the door of that room. "The bad-smelling thing is in there," he said. "Please give me the key."

Now I felt angry. "He's asking too much," I told myself. "I've allowed him to enter my study room, bedroom, sitting room, work room . . . now he wants my last room. No, he needs to realise: He's a *visitor* here. This is *my* house."

He knew what I was thinking. I could see it made him sad.

My anger cooled. I didn't want to make Christ sad. I wanted to do everything he asked. And I knew my life would be better without that rotten thing.

"Lord," I said, "I wish that thing were out of my life, but I do not have the strength to remove it."

"I know you lack strength," he said. "Just give me the key. Give me permission to clean that room, and I will do it."

I gave Christ the key.

He unlocked the door...threw the smelly thing out of the house...and washed the whole room.

How glad I felt to have that rotten sin out of my life!

> When I did not confess my sin,
> my bones rotted....
> Then I confessed my sin to you.
> I stopped hiding it...
> and you forgave my sin. (Psalm 32 [3, 5])

Master of my Whole Heart

Then an exciting thought entered my mind. "Lord," I exclaimed, "you did so well on that locked room; can you please rule my *whole house?*"

"That's exactly what I want to do," he replied. "But I can't rule this house if I'm just a *visitor.*"

Right then I got down on my knees before him and said, "Lord, I've been thinking that I own this house. Beginning today, I choose to recognize you as Master of my whole heart."

Quickly I fetched a paper and wrote, "Christ owns every room of my heart."

What joy I felt as I gave the paper to him!

That day he accepted my entire life . . . all my talents, money, time . . . everything."

After that, I assumed I would just continue staying in the house with Christ. But no! To my surprise, he walked out of the house and down the path.

"Master," I shouted, "I've given you my whole heart. Why are you *leaving* me?"

Looking at me, he said, "I'm not *leaving* you. I'm *leading* you. Come, take my hand. Let's go!"

"Go?" I exclaimed in surprise. *"Go where?"*

"To the world!" he replied. "You have witnessed here in your home area. Now I want you to go to other places—far places—difficult places. You see, there are still nations on earth where few people know me. I want you to go there. I'll go with you. Come with me. Let's go."

I just stood there, looking at him. Then I looked at my house . . . my furniture . . . my comfortable life. Silently I asked myself, "Can I leave all this?"

For a long minute, I didn't move. Then I decided.

Turning my back on the comforts of this world, I ran to join Christ.

Smiling, he put his arm around me as we walked together.

Later he gave me exactly the right wife. She, too, had decided to make Christ the master of every room in her heart.

The road has not been easy. When Christ led us to take the Good News to other nations, I wondered, "Can I quit my job? After spending years getting a degree in Engineering, can I really quit and go...? How will we live?"

On top of that, Carol and I felt heart-broken as we said good-bye to family and friends.

But we love following Jesus.

What joy we feel, seeing people of various nations find new life in Christ; and seeing many of them take the Good News...not only to their own people...but also to people of other languages and nations!

*Invite Christ to be Master of
each room in your heart.
Then go with him,
near and far.*

The End

Christ said,

"The Holy Spirit will fill you with power to witness in Jerusalem, ...and to the ends of the earth." (Acts 1[8])

"Go to every nation. Make disciples. Baptise. Teach them everything I taught you. I am with you until the end of the world." (Matt. 28[19-20])

"This Good News will be preached to every language-group on earth; then the end will come." (Matt. 24[14])

Joanna: My husband seldom talks with me. When I try to talk with him, usually he just remains silent. We both love Christ, but we pray and read God's Word *individually* instead of together.

I feel lonely. Although my husband and I stay in the same house and sleep in the same bed, I feel very alone.

I wish we could be friends. But he thinks it's abnormal for a man to be a friend to his wife.

Our sex is not very exciting. I try to be sexy, but I feel little desire for my husband. Why? Because he wants to be my sex-partner, but not my life-partner.

Note: As Joanna and her husband study pages 7-54 of this book, they will discover that:

As our friendship grows, our sex will improve.

I need you to show your love for me by talking with me as your friend.

I need you to love me with sex.

Men are different from women.

A <u>man</u> can feel sexual desire for his wife, *even if he never talks with her.*

His <u>wife</u> will not feel much sexual desire *unless he communicates with her as a friend.*

Many couples all over the world now realise, "As we build our communication, our love and sex improve."

Hannah: Last week my father died. I felt no sorrow. I have hated him since the day he took my virginity when I was a girl of age 11.

For two years I've been married to a good man. But when we go to bed and he touches me, I suddenly feel nervous and guilty. I feel so *dirty* as I remember what my father did to me.

My husband and I love Christ and we love each other. Will I ever be able to enjoy the sexual part of marriage? How can I change my emotional condition?

Dear Hannah,

Your father did dirty things, but that did not make you dirty. It was his sin, not yours.

Even if you did not say 'no,' it was still 100% his sin. Why? Because you were a child. God will punish any man who does such a thing to a child. (Lev. 18 17, 1 Corinth. 10 8)

Hannah, in God's eyes you are pure.

Believe that you are pure. Believe that sex with your husband is pure, beautiful, enjoyable and holy.

Study Song of Songs 4 11-16. Then, let your husband love you. Encourage him to touch you. Touch him. Be free. Relax. Enjoy. Thank God for marriage. (Prov. 5 18-20)

> The marriage bed is pure. (Heb. 13 4)

Anthony: My wife is young. She doesn't know how to be a wife. Every day I find the house untidy and dinner isn't ready. When we visit my relatives, she isn't polite to them. And she spends money carelessly.

Dear Karunakar,

You can help her to change. How? Be gentle. Don't shout at her. Angry words will never help her to improve.

Here are 3 rules for helping her (or anyone) to improve.

How to change your wife (or your husband)

Rule 1: *Whenever you tell her how she should change, be sure your words are soft and forgiving.*

If you shout at your wife, she will tell herself, "My husband doesn't love me." She will not even think about how she should change. She will just feel unloved and hurt.

But if your words are *soft and forgiving,* she will feel your love, and she will be ready to change. (Proverbs 15 1)

Rule 2: *Give your anger time to cool.*

If tomorrow you feel angry because dinner isn't ready, wait for your anger to cool—after that speak to her about changing. When your anger has cooled, your words can be soft and forgiving.

Rule 3: *Avoid using the word "you."*
Instead, use the words "I feel."

Here are three examples of how to use "I feel" instead of "you."

a) Don't say, *"You* never have dinner ready because you are lazy." Instead, wait for a day when dinner is ready; then say, "Thanks! *I feel* your love when I find dinner ready."

b) Don't say, *"You* are not respectful to my mother because you are impolite and ignorant." That hurts, and doesn't help her to change. Instead say, "Here's how *I feel. I feel* love for you. I also love my mother. My *deepest* love is for you. And *I feel* that you love me when you are kind to my mother."

c) Don't shout, *"You* wasted money on that!" Instead say, *"I feel* hurt when you buy things without discussing it with me. *I feel* close to you when the two of us discuss together what we should buy."

A sentence that begins with *"you"* is hurtful criticism. But if you begin with *"I feel,"* you can share your feelings without pointing a finger at her.

An *"I feel"* sentence helps you to attack the problem, without attacking the person.

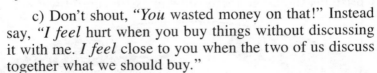

Wives: Use these 3 rules to help your husband to improve.

Joy: At church my husband and I serve on the *"Send-the-Gospel team."* Our church is not rich, but we are working to evangelise people of all languages in our nation, and in two other nations. Please tell us:

> a) Where are the people who have not yet heard of Christ?
> b) What steps can we take to send the gospel to them?

Dear Joy,

Your church listens to the Holy Spirit! Yes, the Holy Spirit gives us the desire to send out the gospel. (Acts 1[8])

a) Where are the people who have not yet heard of Christ?

Today most people who have not heard of Christ live in the areas that are *white* on the map below.

For example:

In Niger there are 20 languages. The people who speak Daza, Dendi, Kanuri, and eight other languages still need to hear the gospel. Missionaries from Nigeria, Ghana, Korea, etc., are witnessing in Niger. More nations should send missionaries there!

In Yemen 95% of the people don't know that Jesus died for sins. Some Christians from Africa, England, India, etc., have jobs in Yemen and witness there. The Yemen government does not give Christians freedom to preach. But more Christians should go there and witness in careful ways.

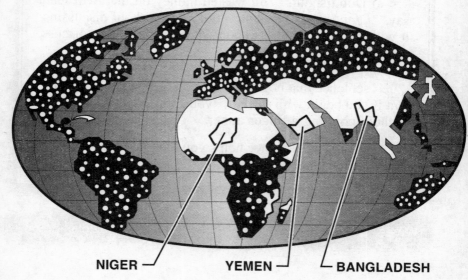

NIGER ⌐   YEMEN ⌐   ⌐ BANGLADESH

Bangladesh has 35 languages. Most of the people have never seen a Bible or heard that Jesus gives eternal life.

b) What steps can you take?

Make a large photocopy of the map on page 140. Colour the white areas *red*. Use the map to show your church which people have not yet heard the Good News.

Teach your church Matt. 28 [18-20]. Also teach the book *Arise Boldly with Power.* [pg 192]

Pray for other nations. (Psa. 67 [1-2])

Trust God to show your church which members to send. (Acts 13 [1-4])

Pray for them.

Give your money to support them. (1 Corinth. 9 [14])

Christ said

"The harvest is large, but the workers are few. Therefore, pray that the Lord will send out workers." (Matt. 9 [37-38])

"Everyone who leaves houses, or brothers, or sisters, or father, or mother...for my sake, will receive much more." (Matthew 19 [29])

"Don't spend your life buying treasures for yourself on earth. Forgiveness of sins must be preached to people of all languages." (Mat. 6 [19], Luke 24 [47])

"I tell you: Open your eyes. The fields are ready for harvest now." (John 4 [35])

Esther: My husband and I are Christians, but daily we argue about money. Bruce and Carol, must a wife beg her husband for money? Or should she have her own money?

Dear Esther,

There are three basic ways that husbands and wives handle money. The first is the "Selfish-Male" way.

1) **Selfish-Male**

In the Selfish-Male way, the man does not tell his wife how much he earns. He keeps it a secret because he plans to spend most of it on himself—not on his wife or children.

Today some wives say, "No. The money I earn is *mine.*"

And sometimes the wife is as selfish as her husband. Then the marriage has endless quarrels.

2) **Both-Selfish**

God's way is better. He says two things about money.

a) *Be generous in giving to the Lord.*

In the Bible God often tells his people: Bring offerings of money, grain, fruit.... (2 Chron. 31 $^{4-8}$, Neh. 10 ^{37}, Neh. 13 $^{12-14}$, Prov. 3 ^{9}, Matt. 6 $^{19-21}$, Acts 20 $^{33-35}$, 1 Corinth. 9 $^{13-14}$, 1 Corinth. 16 ^{2}, 1 Tim. 5 $^{17-18}$, 1 Tim. 6 $^{17-19}$, Heb. 11 ^{26}, 1 Pet. 5 ^{2})

b) *Be generous with each other.*

God says, "A husband must be thoughtful of his wife's needs." (1 Pet. 3 ^{7})

3) God's Way

If a husband wastes all his money on beer, we tell the wife, "Keep your money separate."

But Esther, you and your husband are Christians. So, sit down together and discuss 'money.' If you wish, invite your pastor to join you. Discuss two questions:

     a) How can we give generously to the Lord?
     b) How can we be generous with each other?

Josiah and Sarah: By the middle of each month, our money is finished. Then we quarrel.

Dear Josiah and Sarah,

You need a budget. In fact, every couple needs a budget. A 'budget' is a plan showing: *What we will do with our money each month.*

Budget	
Give to church	13%
food	25%
clothes	5%
housing	20%
transportation	10%
school fees	10%
helping parents	5%
furniture	2%
save in bank	5%
other needs	5%
Our total income	100%

Here's a sample budget made by a husband/wife. Together they decided to give 13% of their monthly income to church.

Then they decided on 25% for food. Why did they pick 25%? Because they noticed that in the previous month they spent 30% on food, but they both said, "We can reduce that to 25%."

Continuing like that, they wrote %'s for each item on their budget.

This couple earned 900 each month. So they gave 900 x 13% = 117 to 'church.' They spent 900 x 25% = 225 on 'food.' They spent 900 x 5% = 45 on 'clothes'....

After a few months, they found, "We must increase our 'transportation' from 10% to 12%. So let's decrease our 'clothes' from 5% to 3%."

In December they spent nothing on 'school fees.' So they banked the 10% until January when fees were due.

To buy furniture, they saved the 2% for many months.

Josiah and Sarah, you should decide together on the %'s you want for church, food, clothes, etc. Of course the total must be 100%. Then, each month be careful not to spend more than the %'s you chose. This will be difficult. It's never easy to stick to a budget. But stick to it. Soon both of you will be saying,

"Since we are careful to be *unselfish,*
and since we stick to our *budget,*
we quarrel less, and we still have money
at the end of the month."

Mary: At the shop, the price of furniture was £299 cash, or
£30 deposit and £16 per month for 24 months.

We calculated that it's better to pay **£299 cash** instead of
£30 plus £16 x 24 = **£414.**

At that time we didn't have £299 cash. So we put money
in the bank each month until we had £299.

We enjoyed showing our children how to calculate the
money we saved. (£414 - £299 = £115 saved)

Dear Mary,

You did well to teach your kids about money. Many
people buy things 'monthly'... then they find, "It's hard to
pay every month." Result: Quarrels in their marriage.

Teach your Kids about Money

Tell your children, "When you begin your own home,
maybe you will have *little* money for furniture. In that case
live without much furniture for some months. Each month
put money in a bank. Then pay ***cash.*** Don't make monthly
payments for furniture (or other things).
Monthly payments are debt. Avoid
debt! You will save money by waiting
until you can pay *cash*.

Make it your aim not to have DEBT

"There are just two things you may
go into debt for: 1) Buying a house.
2) Starting a business.

"Re-pay any debt *quickly.*"

David: I want to give to God's work, but my teacher-salary is small.
By month's end, little money remains for God.

Dear David,

While I was teaching school in Swaziland [for 17 years]
people asked us, "How do you live on one small salary?"

Answer: We are careful how we spend money.

Yet we enjoy life. And we enjoy giving.

Here, David, are 3 excellent rules for giving:

1) When you receive your pay, give part to God *first,* before spending on yourself.

> Give to God the first part of your money/crops. (Prov. 3 [9])

2) Give much. Give *generously!*

> Although the people in Macedonia are very poor, they gave generously, and with joy. (2 Corinth. 8 [1-3])

3) Give so your church can *send* the gospel near and far.

How can people hear without a preacher? How can a preacher go unless he is *sent*? (Rom. 10 [14-15])

A Wife writes

Rachel: As a girl I always hoped for a happy marriage. But now I'm so disappointed.

My husband spends most of his time with his parents. Our house is 10 kms from his parents, yet he spends more time with them, and less time with me and our children.

Sometimes I mention to him that I wish he would spend more time at home, and communicate with me.

He just says, "Don't we sleep in the same bed? My parents brought me up. Shouldn't I care for them now?"

What can I do?

Her Husband writes

Samuel: I'm a successful businessman earning a moderate income.

My wife doesn't want me to visit my parents. She just wants me to spend time with her. She is so possessive of me.

My parents have greater financial needs than her parents. Yet she wants to help hers more than mine.

My marriage-problems bother me so much that now I'm less effective in business.

What's your advice?

Dear Samuel and Rachel,

Here's what God says to you as husband and wife:

Leave your parents.	Care for your parents.
Study Gen. 2 ^{24} and Eph. 5 ^{31}. These verses say: **Leave the home of your parents. Build your own home. Stick to your wife. Love her!**	Study 1 Tim. 5 ^{4} and ^{8}. These verses say: **Love your parents. Find ways to help them— even though you leave their home.**

Samuel, stick to your wife. In the beginning God said, "It's not good for a man to be alone. I will make for him a friend/helper." (Gen. 2 ^{18}) Then God made woman. And God said, "Therefore a man leaves his parents, sticks to his wife, and the two are one." That means: Your wife is your number one relative. And friend.

Rachel, stick to your husband. Respect him. Respect him more than you respect your parents, brothers, or anyone.

Samuel, stick to your wife. Enjoy talking with her about your joys and sorrows. She is your closest friend. If your sister or mother speaks against your wife, just reply, "I love my wife, and I stick to her."

> **Listen mothers: On the day your son marries, let him go. Don't continue holding onto him. Love his wife. If you need clothes, ask his wife. If you went straight to your son, his wife would think, "I'm left out of the relationship between mother and son."**

Rachel, stick to your husband. Admire him. Tell him the things he does well. Do all you can to make him happy. If your relatives speak against your husband, you can reply, "I love and respect my husband."

Samuel and Rachel, be one. Spend time together. Talk freely. Tell each other what makes you happy or sad. Enjoy friendship.

Then the two of you can discuss, *"What should we do for our parents?"* (1 Tim. 5 ^{8}) Continue discussing that question until you reach agreement. After some days if you begin to disagree again, discuss it some more. List

the needs of your parents
(his parents and her parents).
Make a plan to help them.
Never allow anything to
divide you. Stick together.
You are one.

> *Leave your parents. Stick to
> your wife/husband. (Gen. 2 24)
> *Discuss and decide together:
> How will we help and show
> love to your parents and my
> parents? (1 Tim. 5 4 and 8)

Stephen: I'm a pastor. Last week a lady told me that her husband
made a girl pregnant.

I felt shocked. This man was a faithful leader in our church.
I went with one of my deacons to speak to him. He confessed
it's true. And today he confessed it to all the members of our
church.

Now the church is divided.

Some say, "Let's forgive him…and his discipline should be:
For 3 months he will not lead in the church."

Others say, "Let's forgive him…he needs no discipline."
What's your advice?

Dear Stephen,

We say: Forgive him…and his discipline should be:
For a year he will not lead in the church.

Why a *year* instead of 3 months? Because the Bible
strongly forbids adultery. (Heb. 13 4) And the Bible tells
churches to discipline members who fall into sin.

(2 Corinth. 2 6-8 and 1 Tim. 5 20-21)

All church members should realise, "Adultery is serious.
That's why this brother is not allowed to lead for a whole
year. We don't look down on him. We love him. He believes
in Christ. Therefore God has forgiven him. And we forgive
him. Yet a year of discipline is good. Discipline reminds
us all to run from sin." (1 Corinth. 6 18)

> The majority of you agreed to discipline him. That
> discipline is enough. Now forgive and comfort him,
> so that he will not be discouraged by excess sorrow.
> Show him that you still love him. (2 Corinth. 2 6-8)

Another reason for a year [instead of 3 months] is: The brother
needs help—*a year of help*—so that he will not fall into

adultery again. The church should say to two faithful men, "Please meet with this brother for an hour each week to build him up through Bible study and prayer."

After a year of such meetings, the brother should be strong and ready to continue as a leader.

> Brothers, if someone falls into a sin, you who are spiritual must help him back onto the right path. Do it gently. (Gal. 6[1])

Simon: One of our deacons liked to stand up and preach, but last year he divorced his wife and married a very young lady.

We always told him, "Don't do it. Your wife is faithful, never doing adultery."

He didn't seem to care about the problems it brought to his children, or the shame it brought to God's name. He even twisted Bible verses—trying to make his divorce seem okay.

After his divorce and re-marriage, we continued to love him, but we no longer allowed him to preach. So he left and joined a church where he is allowed to preach.

Bruce and Carol, it disturbs me to see a man behave like that.

Dear Simon,

It disturbs us too. Christ said:

> "If a man divorces his wife for any cause except adultery, and marries another lady,
> his sex with her is adultery." (Matthew 19[9])

Malachi chapter 2 says:

14. God sees that you broke your promise to the girl you married when you were young. You promised before God to be faithful to her. She is your partner. But you divorced her.

15. Didn't God make you one flesh and spirit with her...? Let no one break his promise to the wife of his youth.

16. "I hate divorce," says the Lord.... Control your desires. Don't break your promise to be faithful to your wife.

We pray that husbands and wives will:
- *say 'no' to adultery, and 'no' to divorce.*
- *take the effort to improve their marriage.*

[See pages 7 to 54.]

Seth: My wife refuses to respect me. People at church think we have a happy marriage. They don't know how angry she makes me. When I was a boy, I saw my father beat my mother. Now I feel like beating my wife.

Dear Seth,

Don't beat your wife. Instead, do this:
- Sit down with her and explain clearly what she is doing wrong. (Matt. 18 15)
- If she doesn't listen, ask two church-leaders to counsel your wife—and you. (Matt. 18 16)
- Perhaps their counsel will solve the problem. If not, ask your church what action to take. (Matt. 18 17)

In all you do, Seth, show much love and forgiveness to your wife. Study Matt. 18 15-35, especially 18 21-35.

[See also the letter from Philip on page 72.]

Naomi: Our daughter of age two broke my husband's radio. He beat me. Now I'm in hospital.

He attends church with me, but he thinks he's right to beat me.

I know you will tell me, "Be patient." But I'm so tired of being beaten.

Dear Naomi,

No, we are *not* going to tell you, "Be patient."

Instead we say, "Take action."

Yes, we suggest that you take two steps of action:

1) Ask two people [relatives or church-members] to sit down with you and your husband and discuss this issue.

If he won't listen to them, you may report it to the church. (Matt. 18 $^{15\text{-}17}$)

2) Hopefully he will listen to the church. But if he continues beating you, you may need to leave him and stay with relatives, or with a family suggested by your church. Maybe he will change and you can return to him. (1 Corinth. 7 $^{10\text{-}11}$)

Always remember: God is with you, and your church is your helpful family. (Psalm 31 and Gal. 6 ^{2})

Deborah: I had to leave my husband. He beat me such that my life was in danger.

Since the day I left him, some people at church look down on me, like I'm no longer a 1st class Christian, but 3rd class.

The Bible says, "A wife should not leave her husband, but if she does, she must remain single, or return to him." (1 Cor. 7 $^{10\text{-}11}$) I will obey that. I doubt that I can ever return to my husband, but I won't re-marry and I won't have sex. I just want to work for Christ.

Dear Deborah,

We are glad that you want to obey 1 Corinth. 7 $^{10\text{-}11}$.

Maybe God will do a miracle so that you can return to your husband. If not, continue saying 'no' to adultery, even when you feel a longing to have someone to talk to and sleep with. Serve Christ with all your heart. (2 Tim. 4 $^{7\text{-}8}$)

Hannah: Five years ago my husband left me and began staying with a girl. Daily she put pressure on him to divorce me.

Months passed . . . horrible, dreadful months. Whenever I tried to phone my husband, she answered the phone. She laughed at me, and never let me speak to him.

I told myself, "Nobody loves me. I just want to die!"

Yet my Bible reading helped me to trust God. And the women of our church encouraged me.

After a year my husband came back to me!

God helped me to accept him with loving arms.

The church said that an elder must spend time counselling him, and he must be tested for HIV. That was hard for him to accept. But now our marriage is good. How glad I am that I didn't divorce!

Hannah did well not to divorce.
Her letter also reminds us to tell everyone: *Run away from adultery*. Adultery brings *sorrow* to a home. (Gal. 6[7])

Luke: At my church, how can I teach people about marriage?

Dear Luke,

Start by teaching Eph. 5 [22-33]. Those verses say, "Submit to your husband." That means: Don't try to be his boss. Respect him. Love him.

Eph. 5 [22-33] also says, "Love your wife." That means: Be kind. Help her with the work at home. Talk with her as your friend.

After you teach Eph. 5 [22-33], you can invite adults to a meeting where they are free to ask questions about marriage and singleness.

These verses will help you to answer their questions.

VERSES ON MARRIAGE AND SINGLENESS

No sex before marriage
1 Thes. 4 [3-8]
1 Tim. 5 [1-2], 2 Tim. 2 [22]
Deut. 22 [13-29]

Marry a believer
2 Corinth. 6 [14]

Church-leaders
1 Tim. 3, Titus 1 [6]

Respect, love, sex
1 Pet. 3 [1-7], Tit. 2 [4]
Col. 3 [5-10, 12-19]
1 Corinth. 7 [3-5]
Song of Sg. 4 [10-16]

Widows
1 Corinth. 7 [39-40]
1 Tim. 5 [3-16]

No sex with kids....
Lev. 18 [6-18], 20 [10-12]

No adultery, divorce
Matt. 5 [31-32], 19 [3-9]
1 Corinth. 7 [10-16]

Church discipline
1 Corinth. 5
2 Corinth. 2 [6]

Joy: I'm age 28. I have two children. My husband died 4 years ago. This year I started praying for a husband. Then I met John. He's a sweet, considerate man. He believes in God, but he's not a Christian. I mean, he has never decided to receive Christ as his Saviour. He takes me to church services, but he himself doesn't enter the house of God.

I believe God is answering my prayer for a husband, but God is giving me a non-Christian. I don't complain. I just hope that after we marry, I will be able to mould him.

Dear Joy,

The Bible says: You are free to marry. (1 Tim. 5 [14]) But if you marry, the man must be a real Christian.

> A woman is tied to her husband until he dies.
> Then she is free to marry again,
> but only to a man who is in the Lord.
> (1 Corinth. 7 [39])
> Do not yoke yourselves with unbelievers.
> (2 Corinth. 6 [14])

Joy, don't say, "God is giving me a non-Christian." God never goes against the Bible.

Do this. Obey the Bible. Remain single, or marry a true Christian.

All of the Bible is breathed by God. Teach it to people. The Bible will correct their errors, and train them to live right. (2 Tim. 3 [16])

Yes, obey the Bible yourself…then teach your children to obey it. Every day sit down with them, sing together, read the Bible, discuss it, and do it! (Deut. 6 [6-7]) Here are some good verses.

Become a Christian. Psa. 51 [2-3], John 3 [16], Romans 10 [9-10].

Study your Bible. Joshua 1 [8], Acts 17 [11].

Hell … Heaven. Luke 16 [24], Rev. 20 [15].

Help orphans widows. Mat. 25 [35-40], Ja. 2 [15-16], 1 Jn. 3 [17-18]

Obey. God protects. 2 Chron. 7 [13-14], Psalm 5 [12], 34 [15-16], 66 [18-19], 97 [10].

Be honest at work. Dan. 6 [4], Isaiah 33 [15], 2 Chron. 19 [7].

Beer. Isa. 5 [11, 12, 22], Prov. 20 [1], Eph. 5 [18].

False prophets. Deut. 13 [1-5], Matt. 7 [15-23].

Church Leaders: Our church has more than ten women who have non-believing husbands. As leaders, we want to help them. Please answer our 3 questions.

1) What does the Bible say to wives of unbelieving husbands?

2) How can the church help unbelieving husbands to believe?

3) Can we tell wives, "Have faith; sooner or later your husband will choose to believe."?

Dear Leaders,

1) What does the Bible say to wives of unbelieving husbands?

> Each wife must respect her husband.
> If a wife has an unbelieving husband,
>   she may win him by her behaviour.
> She will not need to say any words,
>   because he will see her pure life. (1 Peter 3 1-2)

Notice those verses do *not* say, "A wife should preach loud and long to her husband." Instead they say: she may win him by her *'behaviour'* without any *'words.'*

To preach many *words* would be easy. But to *behave* right—that's difficult—especially at home!

At home people see how we behave. They see what we do when other people criticize us wrongly. They notice if we work hard even when no one says, "Thanks."

The key that helps husbands to accept Christ is:
Wife's behaviour at home.

Abel told us, "I didn't want to listen when my wife told me how she accepted Jesus. I got angry when she said that Jesus could save me from my sins. I got more angry when she put a Bible on my chair. But then one day when she had done something wrong, she said, 'Sorry.' (In our previous years of marriage, she had *never* said, 'Sorry.') That day I realised:

"She really has Jesus. And I need Jesus."

2) How can the church help unbelieving husbands to believe?

Recently I [Carol] joined other ladies in planning a

'Couples Dinner.' We invited husbands and wives. Many of the husbands were unbelievers.

As couples arrived the chairman welcomed each one warmly. Soon the unbelievers began to relax. They realised, "No one is going to point a finger at me and preach at me."

After a delicious dinner, a soccer-star stood up to tell the story of his life. In a friendly way he told how he got into sports, and how he decided to accept Christ. His voice didn't sound like preaching. He simply told his story. Everyone listened with interest.

He ended with, "On your table are some small papers. Take one now. Write on it your name and phone number. Put a ✓ if you want me to phone you tomorrow. Then the two of us can arrange to meet so that I can explain how you can receive Christ."

Sixteen men put a ✓. Praise God!

That's one way to reach husbands. Here's another:

Some members of your church can plan a 'Marriage Discussion' where couples can discuss a topic such as:

a) Money handling in marriage. [pages 142-145]

b) Interesting differences between men and women. [pg 99]

c) It's important to satisfy your husband/wife. [pgs 35-41]

d) How your children can avoid HIV. [pages 115-120]

Especially invite couples where the husband (or the wife) isn't a believer.

Meet in a home—not in church. In the meeting, make unbelievers feel relaxed. Avoid church-words. Don't have a 'service.' Drink tea and be normal people at home.

One Christian man can be the 'Discussion Leader.' If the topic is 'Money handling,' he can encourage everyone to give his/her ideas on money-in-marriage.

When an unbeliever says his ideas, don't jump on him with, "But we Christians believe...." Be gentle. Be friendly. Help everyone to enjoy the discussion.

Probably many will want to meet again every week.

After several weeks, the Discussion Leader can end by saying,

"Let me take just six minutes to tell you:

1) How my life was <u>before</u> I received Christ.

2) <u>How</u> <u>I</u> <u>received</u> <u>Christ</u>. [pages 29-30]

3) How my life is changing <u>now</u>."

"After this meeting, I will be glad to speak with those of you who would like to receive Christ."

3) Can you promise a wife, "Sooner or later your husband will believe."?

No. Some husbands decide to take Christ; others decide not to. (1 Corinth. 7 16) Here are three true stories.

a) Martha's husband refused to believe. And he began having sex with girls. Martha realised, "I'm in danger of getting HIV from him." So she had to leave him and stay with a family recommended by her church. [page 38]

b) Rhoda says, "My husband was a good man. We were married 23 years. I prayed for him every day. Often he told me, 'Since the day you received Christ, I like the way you respect me...but as for me, I will never be a Christian.' When he died, I was sorry that he went to hell. But I realised: It was not my fault or my choice."

c) Andrew says, "I didn't like to see my wife reading her Bible. Then one day she told me, 'By reading this, I've seen how I can be right with God.' That started me thinking. Six years later I accepted Christ. I know she was praying for me daily."

Serve God

If your husband is an unbeliever, he may not allow you to do certain things, but you can still find ways to serve God.

In the Bible we find women who did much for God,

even if their husbands were not Christians. Two examples are:

a) Esther's husband was an un-believer, yet she helped people in 127 countries. (Esther 4 [16] and 9 [29-30])

> **All over the world women with unsaved husbands are finding ways to serve Christ.**

b) Acts 16 [1] indicates that Timothy's mother was married to an un-believer. Yet Timothy became a man of God because of his mother and grandmother. (2 Tim. 1 [5] and 3 [15])

Yes, ladies, if your husband doesn't believe, you can still serve God, and you can train your children/grandchildren to serve God!

Priscilla: I'm age 33 and not married. One man loves me. Daily he comes to my flat and we enjoy sex.

But he has a wife.

At the office where I work the Christians meet every noon. Today they helped me to receive Christ. I'm happy, but I'm *afraid* to tell 'my man.' He's the only man I have. How can I say 'no' to him; after all we've done to each other. He will get *terribly angry!*

Dear Priscilla,

The Holy Spirit now lives in you. With his power you can tell this married man, "I've made the great choice. I've chosen Christ. He's my Lord. So I will no longer have sex outside marriage."

Then tell him how he can get eternal life. [page 27-28]

All over the world people who receive Christ speak boldly like that.

You can too.

> **God did not give us the spirit of fear, but of power, love, and self-control.** (2 Tim. 1 [7])

(Read the book *Arise Boldly with Power.* It has a chapter that shows how you can help a person to accept Christ. See page 192.)

Gladys: In your book *Love & Marriage,* you say, "Most young people secretly feel sad because they think, 'I'm useless.'" How can I help my son (age 13) to avoid that feeling?

Dear Gladys,

In every nation on earth many teenagers say:

"Yes, I feel useless. Why? Because I'm not intelligent. My sister does well in school. I don't.

"And I'm hopeless in sports.

"On top of that: I'm ugly. At home and at school, people call me names and laugh at me. Everyone looks down on me. I have no true friends. I wish I'd never been born."

On the surface, young people appear happy. They laugh and play with their friends. But under the surface, many of them are terribly sad.

Even excellent students think, "Other kids are smart, but I'm not."

And no matter how nice-looking they are, nearly all of them hate their own body for being 'too tall,' or 'too fat,' or 'too . . . .'

Gladys, it's good that you want to help your son not to feel useless. Here's how a parent can help a teenage son or daughter:

parent: Who is the most happy kid at school?

teenager: Probably Simon.

parent: Why do you say he's happy?

teenager: He laughs a lot.

parent: Does he like to point at another kid and laugh at his clothes and the shape of his head?

teenager: Yes. How did you know?

parent: Tell me, why does Simon do that? Is it possible that deep in his heart he feels sad and useless?

teenager: No, not Simon. He's always happy.

parent: Are you sure? Think carefully about *why* he laughs at the weak points of other kids.

That discussion will start your child thinking, "Do some kids actually feel sad; even though they laugh often?"

On another day, continue the discussion like this:

parent: Do you realise that as kids grow up, most of them go through some years of feeling useless? In fact, sooner or later, you yourself will probably feel that way.

teenager: I feel that way *now!* I didn't tell you because I thought you wouldn't understand.

parent: If you do these two things, you will not feel useless.

1) Worry less about *your* needs; consider the needs of *others*.

Tell yourself, "I must help Simon. Probably he laughs at other kids because he himself feels useless. I can encourage him."

Then look for opportunities to compliment him. If he makes a mistake in soccer, don't laugh. Point out the things he did well.

You will find that Simon is not the only one who needs your encouragement. God will use you to build up many kids. And as you are busy building them up, some of them will become your true friends. They will encourage you.

2) Remember how much God loves *you*.

God gave the blood of his Son so that you can enter heaven. Yes, he loves *you*. And he has work for you to do here on earth. You aren't useless.

Ten years from now you can be serving God in some great way, such as planting churches in a place where people don't know Christ.

For now, you can serve God right in your school.

Some of your friends may tell you, "At home nobody loves me. My parents never wanted me. I'm just an accident."

You can reply, "You're not an accident. Every human is planned by God. Accept Christ. Serve him with the talents he has given you. You aren't useless!" (Jer. 1⁵⁻⁸)

Lois: I'm age 23; and I'm not sure whether I want to marry or remain single. Must every Christian young person marry?

Dear Lois,

Every Christian young person should have the attitude:

*I will spend my life
doing all I can to spread the Good News
to the people of my own nation
and to other nations.
I will marry only if marriage will help me to
serve Christ better.*

Today in countries such as Libya, Turkey, Iran, Somalia, China . . . there are millions of people who have never seen a church that speaks their language, and they have never heard how to receive eternal life. Let's encourage our churches to send out true Christians who will tell them of hope in Christ.
Let's PRAY.   Let's GIVE.   Let's be willing to GO.

PRAY

"The harvest is huge. Pray that God will send out more workers."
(Matt. 9 [37-38])

GIVE

"Don't spend your life buying treasures on earth."
(Matt. 6 [19])

"Give with joy.
(2 Corinth. 9 [7])

GO

God commanded us, "Bring salvation to all the earth."
(Acts 13 [47])

"Lord, send me."
(Isaiah 6 [8])

Single: Some Christians may decide, "I can serve Christ better if I remain single. As a single person I will have no responsibility to a husband/wife. I will be whole-hearted for Christ." (1 Corinth. 7 ³²⁻³⁵)

Married: Other Christians may decide, "I would like to marry a really diligent Christian so that we can serve Christ *together.*" (Psalm 34 ³)

Lois, do this. Read the book: *Arise Boldly with Power.* Serve Christ with zeal! Then, marry only if marriage will help you to serve Christ better.

Muriel: I love teaching school. The headmaster and parents often say how much they appreciate me. But I always hate to go home to my husband. All he does is criticize me. No matter how carefully I cook, he complains that the meat isn't right, or his tea is too strong....

What can I do so he will begin to appreciate me?

Dear Muriel,

a) Discuss it with your husband. With respectful words, let him know how much you need his appreciation. This will be hard for you to say, but say it!

b) Realise that your husband needs appreciation too. Some men act like they don't need appreciation, but they definitely need it! [See page 29.] Muriel, show much appreciation to your husband; then it will be easier for him to appreciate you.

Elijah: Do drugs such as cocaine (crack) improve sex?

Dear Elijah,

No. Men who use such drugs often find that their penis can no longer get hard. Women who use drugs give birth to babies that are crippled.

God's way is better than drugs. His way is:

Love your wife.   *Enjoy* her. Let her
Be faithful to her.   love satisfy you.
  (Eph. 5 ³³)   (Prov. 5 ¹⁸⁻²¹)

Angela: I heard ladies at church say, "If a wife does the 'PC exercise,' she and her husband will find more pleasure in sex." Is that true? Does that exercise really help?

Dear Angela,

Yes, every wife should do the 'PC exercise.' Why?

a) It will help her and her husband to enjoy sex more.

b) This exercise makes childbirth safer for mother and baby.

Is your PC strong or weak?

A woman's PC muscle controls her bladder and vagina. If her PC muscle is strong, her vagina will hold her husband's penis tightly. This will help her to feel pleasure during sex. [See Picture 1.]

If her PC muscle is weak, her vagina will be loose. Then she will fail to find much pleasure in sex. [See Picture 2.]

Many women have a loose vagina [Picture 2]. Why? Because they don't know how to exercise their PC muscle.

When a woman is told, "Your PC muscle needs exercise," she may not know how to do it. For example, when Esther began trying to exercise her PC, she made the mistake of squeezing the wrong muscle. Every time she told herself, "Now I will squeeze my PC," she actually squeezed her thigh muscles instead.

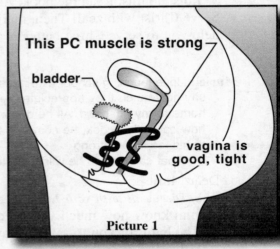

This PC muscle is strong

bladder

vagina is good, tight

Picture 1

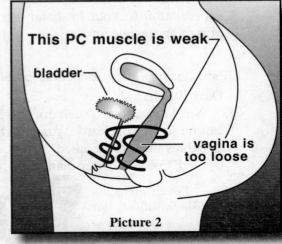

This PC muscle is weak

bladder

vagina is too loose

Picture 2

In only 7 days, you can learn to squeeze your PC muscle

For the next 7 days, practise squeezing your PC each time you pass urine. Why urine? Because the PC controls two things: the vagina and the bladder. [picture 1]

Do this. For the next week, each time you urinate, spread your knees far apart . . . start passing urine . . . then stop it for a few seconds . . . then start it . . . then stop it again for a few seconds. Continue to start-stop, start-stop until your bladder is empty. *Each time you stop the urine, you are squeezing your PC muscle.*

Why must your knees be far apart? Because, if your knees were close together, you could stop urine with your thigh muscles. But with your knees far apart, only the PC can stop it.

Practise 'start-stop' for 7 days. Then you will know how to squeeze your PC. And you will find, "I can squeeze my PC *at any time* [not only while passing urine]."

After the 7 days, begin doing this 'PC exercise' every day

PC exercise

a) Squeeze your PC tightly . . . continue squeezing for 2 seconds.

b) Relax it . . . remain relaxed for 3 seconds.

Do that 40 times each day.

Yes, every woman should do the 'PC exercise' 40 times each day.

It's easy. Every morning before you get out of bed, do the exercise ten times. (That means: Squeeze for 2 seconds; relax for 3 seconds . . . repeat that ten times.)

Then do about five exercises while eating breakfast, another ten at lunch . . . and so on until you reach 40 by the end of the day. (Since the PC is inside your body, no one can see when you are squeezing it.)

Rhoda often forgot to do 40 exercises each day. So she

wrote 'PC exercise' on little papers, and put one paper on her mirror, another on her stove, and so on. One day her sister saw the papers and asked, "PC exercise???"

So Rhoda told her how to do PC exercises. Two months later her sister returned saying, "My husband loves the way I enjoy sex now. He asked, 'What *medicine* did your sister give you?'"

> **Why does the PC exercise help? Answer: A wife with a strong PC can squeeze her husband's penis during sex. That helps her to enjoy sex.**

Americans were not first

In 1978 Americans discovered the PC exercise. They think they were the first to discover it. The truth is: For hundreds of years many people in Asia and Africa have had a custom that a girl may not marry until she is able to squeeze her vagina (PC) tightly. Another Asian/African custom is: After a wife has a baby, she exercises her vagina (PC) so that it gets strong again.

To every wife on earth we say:

Learn to squeeze your PC.
Then do the 'PC exercise' 40 times each day.
That will make childbirth more safe, and it will
bring you and your husband extra pleasure in sex.

Christine: I'm pregnant. My husband wants to know:
  a) Must we stop having sex in month 6, or 7... or when?
  b) After childbirth, how many weeks must we wait before we begin sex again?

Dear Pavithra,

a) **Do not have sex during month 9.**
   Have sex freely in months 1 to 8.
      Yes, even in month 8 when your stomach is large, you and your husband can find positions for sex that cause you no pain. [page 97]

During pregnancy a woman's clitoris is extra excitable. Therefore, a wife will find extra pleasure in sex during pregnancy. God planned it that way. God's plan is:

> During pregnancy a husband and wife
> should find *extra joy in sex*.
> That makes their *love grow*.
> Then the baby is born into a
> *home filled with love*.

b) Sex after childbirth:

Wait about 3 weeks after childbirth, then continue sex. Your doctor will tell you if you should wait more than 3 weeks.

Sarah: I'm pregnant. People tell me, "Men can't live without sex. In the weeks ahead, your husband will chase girls—until the day you can start giving him sex again."

I hate the thought of adultery. What can I do?

Dear Sarah,

It's not true that men can't live without sex.

God commands men and women to have self-control. (Titus 2 [11-12])

Listen, Sarah, while you are pregnant, help your husband in two ways:

> **God does not believe that, "Men can't live without sex." God knows men. He made men. And he commands men: Don't have sex before marriage, and be faithful in marriage.**
> (Gen. 39 [9], Prov. 5 [18-21] and 7 [7-25])

1) Enjoy sex with him often, until the end of month 8. After that, he should not enter your vagina during month 9, and for about 3 weeks after childbirth.

During those 7 weeks, find ways to satisfy him. Since he should not enter your vagina, satisfy him with your thighs, or hand, or...whatever ways <u>both</u> of you enjoy. Satisfy him often.

2) Don't get so busy caring for your baby that you forget to show concern for your husband. Don't let your husband feel replaced by a baby. Be careful to show much love to him, even though you are excited about your baby.

> **Husband: If you do adultery, God will *never* say, "It's not your fault...it's your wife's fault."**
> **If you do adultery, it's *your* sin. Study Ezekiel 18 [20].**

Miriam: I'm four months pregnant. My husband still wants sex, but I fear that his sperm will harm the baby inside me.

Dear Miriam,

Enjoy sex with your husband.

Don't worry. When a woman gets pregnant, a **plug** forms. The plug prevents sperm from reaching the baby.

Continue sex until the end of month 8. He should not enter your vagina in month 9, and for about 3 weeks after childbirth. During those weeks, find ways to satisfy him with your thighs, hand, or....

Enjoy satisfying each other. That joy will help you and your husband to grow in love. And that's good because every baby needs a love-filled home.

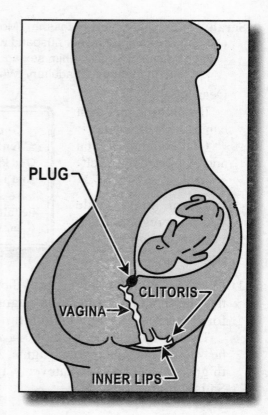

PLUG

CLITORIS

VAGINA →

INNER LIPS

Ethel: On the day I discovered I was pregnant, I stopped drinking and smoking. But now my baby is crippled...just because of my drinking/smoking. I want to tell every woman: Never drink or smoke.

Listen every lady on earth: Alcohol, tobacco, or drugs can harm a baby-embryo in the *first month* of pregnancy; before you realise you are pregnant. Therefore, never drink, smoke, or use drugs. And never tell yourself, "When I find I'm pregnant, then I will stop drinking." That's too late.

Mary: I'm not HIV+, but I fear to breast-feed my baby because my breasts are small, and my milk appears weak. Is the milk sold in shops better than my breast-milk?

Dear Mary,

No, the milk sold in shops is *not* better.

Breast-feed your baby.

It doesn't matter if your breasts are small. Small breasts make as much milk as big ones. And don't worry if your milk seems weak. Breast-milk appears thin, but it's the best milk for a baby.

Note: If a mother is HIV+, her breast-milk contains HIV. So, a woman who is HIV+ should ask a doctor/nurse, "How can I avoid passing HIV to my baby?"

Jane: Recently I had a baby. Now my husband wants to make me pregnant as soon as possible.

But isn't it good for a woman to have a space of 2 years between pregnancies?

Dear Jane,

Yes, a space of at least two years helps the *mother,* and it helps the *children.*

Mothers are more healthy if they have a two-year-space between pregnancies. If the space is only one year, the mother may become weak, or even ill.

Children are stronger if there is a space of two or three years between them.

Elliot: Today my wife told me, "Now that I have a baby, please stay in your own bed. After two years you can make me pregnant again."

I told her, "I don't want two years of no sex. Let's use family planning."

Dear Elliot,

You are correct. A wife should never tell her husband, "No sex for two years."

God tells husbands and wives:

> Continue satisfying each other's sex-needs.
> (1 Corinth. 7 [5])

You and your wife should:

a) Continue enjoying sex with each other.

b) Use family planning to avoid pregnancy (for two years) so that her body can build up strength before she gets pregnant again.

There are many methods of family planning. We recommend, 'Natural Family Planning.' This method can be used in two ways.

1) To avoid pregnancy: You can use Natural Family Planning to avoid pregnancy—in order to put a space of two years (or more) between pregnancies.

2) To help her get pregnant: If a wife is not getting pregnant, Natural Family Planning may help her to get pregnant.

If you want to avoid pregnancy, <u>or</u> if you want to get pregnant, read pages 169-181. Those pages explain Natural Family Planning.

Joel: My wife doesn't get pregnant. I work in town. Every weekend I go home and we have sex often — yet no baby.

Dear Joel,

Let us explain 'Natural Family Planning.'

Each month a woman has only a *few* days when getting pregnant is possible. Those *few* days are called her 'Baby Days.'

Your wife should learn to recognize her Baby Days.

Then she can say to you, "Today is one of my Baby Days. Let's have sex today."

Then, after she has a baby, she may say, "You and I decided that I should not get pregnant again for 2 years. Today is <u>not</u> a Baby Day. So let's enjoy sex today!"

How can she know which days are Baby Days? She must just notice what her body is doing each day.

A woman's body does this:

Each month she has blood for a few days.

After that her vagina produces a little 'mucus.'

So, every month there are *two* liquids — first blood; then mucus.

All women know about the blood, but some women fail to notice the mucus.

Mucus is a colourless liquid — like the colourless liquid in a raw egg.

When a woman decides, "I will be careful to notice what my body does each day," she will find that:

After my bleed-days, my 'inner lips' [page 46] feel dry. Then, after a few days, my 'inner lips' change to wet. That's mucus. The amount of mucus is so small; I cannot see it. But I feel it.

The mucus makes my 'inner lips' feel wet and slippery. It feels like those lips are wet with the clear liquid of an egg. I feel it as I walk. I feel it all day... for a few days.

Then the mucus disappears. My inner lips feel dry for about two weeks. Then my bleed-days come again.

Why should a wife know about mucus? For this reason:
A woman can easily get pregnant on her mucus days,
because sperm easily move through mucus.

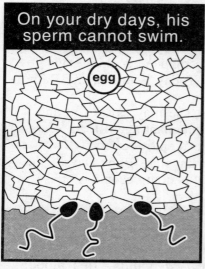

If a man has sex with his wife on
a day when she has no mucus,
his sperm will go nowhere, and
she will not get pregnant.

If they have sex on a mucus day,
his sperm will move through her
mucus and possibly reach her egg
and make her pregnant.

Question 1: "Does mucus make me feel wet *inside my vagina?*"
    No. Mucus makes you feel wet on your 'inner lips' that
are *outside your vagina.* [page 46] The inside of your vagina
is always wet (like inside your mouth). But your 'inner
lips' feel dry on certain days, and wet on other days. When
those lips feel wet, that's mucus.

Question 2: "When I kiss my husband, I get excited and my
'inner lips' feel wet. Is that mucus?"
    No, that's not mucus. On mucus days your inner lips feel
wet *every hour of the day* — not just when you kiss.

    Happy is the woman who knows her mucus days. She
can say to her husband,

"When we want a baby, I know on which days we should have sex. And when we don't want a pregnancy, I know the days on which we can freely have sex... without me getting pregnant."

Unfortunately, many women don't have that knowledge. The only thing they know is, "Each month I have some bleed-days. I don't know about mucus. I don't know on which days I can get pregnant. If I have sex today, could I get pregnant?... I don't know."

Such ignorance is terrible. Women need knowledge!

Here's the Knowledge Women Need

◆ **A woman's menstrual-cycle begins with about five bleed-days.**

◆ **After that, her inner lips usually turn dry, and remain dry for a few days.**

◆ **Then (for about five days) her inner lips feel wet all day. She knows, "These are my mucus days."**

◆ **After the mucus days, her inner lips turn dry again, and remain dry for about two weeks.**

◆ **Then her next bleed-days begin.**

A woman's big question is: On which days can I get pregnant?

Answer: You can get pregnant on your mucus days, and the 3 days after your last mucus day.

Your 'Baby Days' are:
a) all of your mucus days, and
b) the 3 days after your last mucus day.

To get pregnant, do this: After your bleed-days, notice each day whether your inner lips are dry or wet with mucus. Then, each evening write the word 'dry' or 'mucus' on a chart [photocopy page 173].

The chart below was made by a lady named Ruth. We see that this time her 'menstrual-cycle' was 27 days. Maybe her next 'cycle' will be 30 days . . . or 20 days. That doesn't matter. She makes a new chart for each cycle. And her 'Baby Days' are always:

      a) her mucus days, and

      b) the 3 days following her last mucus day.

A woman can get pregnant on any of her Baby Days, but the 'best days' for getting pregnant are:

      1) the last day of mucus ('very wet mucus' day).

      2) the next day ('nearly dry' day).

Since Ruth wants to get pregnant, she and her husband should be sure to have sex on her two 'best days.'

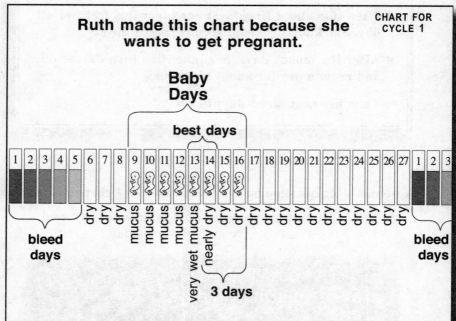

Ruth made this chart because she wants to get pregnant.

CHART FOR CYCLE 1

Baby Days

best days

bleed days

very wet mucus • nearly dry • **3 days**

bleed days

To get pregnant, Ruth should have sex on any 'Baby Day,' and especially on her two 'best days.'

Natural Family Planning
(Photocopy this page; then make your own charts.)

After your bleed-days, each evening write a word such as 'dry' or 'mucus' on your chart. [See pages 172 and 177.]

Remember: 'Baby Days' are all of your mucus days, plus the 3 days after your last mucus day.

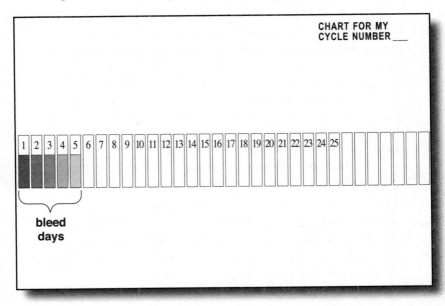

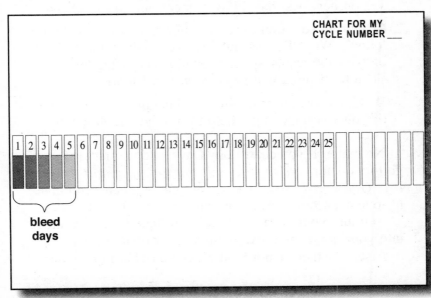

Joel, everything we have told you is called 'Natural Family Planning.' Here is how you can use Natural Family Planning to help your wife get pregnant.

● For every menstrual-cycle your wife should make a chart similar to Ruth's chart on page 172.

It's difficult for a woman to make her *first* chart. Often she may wonder, "Are my inner lips wet, or dry?"

Encourage your wife not to give up. Making the first chart seems difficult, but after that it becomes easy.

Joel, you can do one thing to help her. During all the days when she is making her *first* chart, don't have sex. Why? Because sex makes her inner lips wet, and then she will not be sure, "Today are my lips wet from mucus, or wet from sex?"

So, Joel, for only about 30 days (while she is making her first chart) don't have sex.

● After that first chart, your wife will continue to make a chart for each cycle. You will be happy when she says, "Let's have sex . . . it's a Baby Day." And a few days later she will say, "Today and tomorrow are my 'best days.' Darling, let's *enjoy* these two days!"

● Try to find a way to stay together. You can't have sex on her 'best days' if you meet only on weekends.

● During sex, don't use any lubricant (such as 'body lotion'). Why? Because lubricants can kill sperm. Instead of using lubricants, spend a long time enjoying loveplay. Then her vagina will produce *natural* lubrication.

● After a year, if your wife is still not pregnant, you may (if you wish) try to get help from a qualified doctor.

No matter if you chart Baby Days, and no matter if you go to a doctor—*your wife will not get pregnant unless it is <u>God's</u> will.* So, if she never gets pregnant, continue to love each other. And continue to serve God together.

You and your wife may decide to take homeless kids into your home, and love them as your own. (Ja. 1 27)

Also, whether or not God gives you children, be sure

to do this: *As husband and wife, use your time and money to spread the Good News both near and far.*
(Luke 24 [47], Rom. 15 [20])

PRAY...GIVE...GO

Joel: I have a question. In your letter you say,

    a) Baby Days are 'mucus days,'
      and
    b) 'the 3 days after her last mucus day.'

I don't understand part b).
How can she get pregnant '3 days after her last mucus day'?

Dear Joel,

It's like this. A farmer waits for rain. Then, when the soil is wet, he begins planting little onion plants. As the rains continue, each day he plants more onions in the wet soil. When the rains stop, he continues planting for 3 days. Those days seem dry, but the soil remains wet for 3 days.

Joel, you can do the same. Put sperm in your wife on her mucus days, and for 3 days after mucus. The days after mucus seem dry, but some mucus remains for 3 days.

> The next year Joel's wife gave birth to a baby girl. Then Joel wrote:

Joel: We are so happy for our girl. Now we want to give her two years to grow strong. Then we hope to have another child. So, for the next two years, we don't want a pregnancy.

To avoid pregnancy, I think we must never have sex on her Baby Days, but we can have sex on her 'safe' days.

By 'safe' I mean, 'Days when she cannot get pregnant.'

Dear Joel,

You are wise to want 'two years' between pregnancies. Yes, you can avoid pregnancy by having sex on her 'safe' days. Do this:

Your wife should continue making a chart for each cycle,

but now (since she wants to avoid pregnancy) she must mark her charts differently. See the chart on page 177.

Notice on that chart there are *two* kinds of safe days: 'Early Safe Days' and 'Late Safe Days.'

On 'Late Safe Days' the husband and wife are free to have sex as often as they wish.

'Early Safe Days' are different. On page 177 notice the 'Rules for Early Safe Days.'

To avoid pregnancy, a woman must understand just three things:

1) Early Safe Days: After your 'bleed-days,' usually your inner lips will feel dry for some days. Those dry days are 'Early Safe Days.' You may have sex on those days, but follow the two 'Rules for Early Safe Days.' [page 177]

2) Baby Days: After some days you will notice, "Today my inner lips feel wet." The wet feeling will continue for about five days. On each wet-day, write the word 'mucus' on your chart. *To avoid pregnancy, never have sex on 'mucus' days. And when the mucus stops, continue to avoid sex for 3 more days.*
The 'mucus days' plus '3 days' are your 'Baby Days.'

3) Late Safe Days: There are <u>no</u> rules for 'Late Safe Days.' On these days, enjoy sex with your husband often…at any time.
'Late Safe Days' continue for nearly two weeks. Then your next 'bleed-days' will begin.

To avoid pregnancy, Ruth and her husband have sex on 'Safe Days,' never on 'Baby Days.'

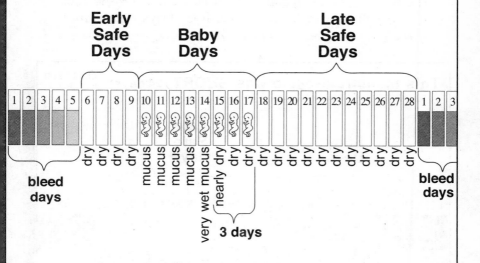

On 'Early Safe Days' follow the two Rules. [See below.]
  On 'Baby Days' avoid sex.
    On 'Late Safe Days' enjoy sex anytime . . . and often!

Rules for Early Safe Days

Rule 1: On 'Early Safe Days' you may have sex in the evening, but not in the morning.

Why? Because sex in the morning makes the inner lips feel wet all day, and then it's difficult for the wife to know when her mucus arrives.

Rule 2: On 'Early Safe Days' do not have sex two days in a row. Skip at least one day in between.

Why? Because if a wife has sex every evening, her inner lips will feel wet all the time, and so she will not know when her mucus arrives.

Your charts may be long or short

A woman may have a cycle of 32 days, and then one of 24 days…that doesn't matter. For each cycle she makes a new chart [using page 173]. After her 'bleed-days,' each day she writes 'dry' or 'mucus' on her new chart. As she does so, she will see which days are her Baby Days — *no matter if the chart becomes 24 days, or 28 days, or 32, or….*

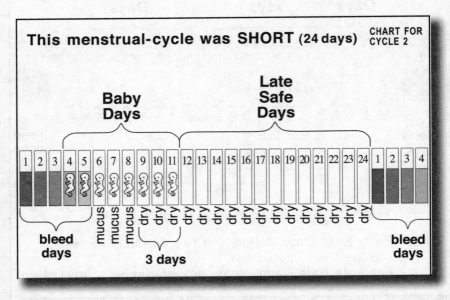

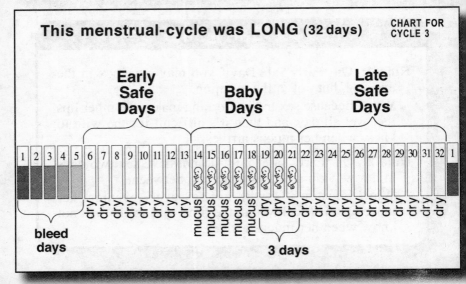

After childbirth

During pregnancy a woman doesn't need to make charts. After childbirth she should begin making charts so that she can avoid getting pregnant again too soon.

Her *first* chart after childbirth will be *unusual*. Why? Because after childbirth her inner lips will be dry for perhaps 50 days, or 100 days, or more. So her first chart will have *many* 'Early Safe Days.'

To all wives we say: Three weeks after you give birth, begin making a chart [like the one below]. During your many 'Early Safe Days' obey the 'Rules' [page 177]. Then, sooner or later, you will begin having mucus days. Avoid sex on those 'Baby Days.' Then you and your husband can enjoy sex freely during your 'Late Safe Days.'

After that, your charts will return to normal...they will be about 30 days each. By making a chart for each menstrual-cycle, you can succeed in avoiding pregnancy for two years, or more if you wish.

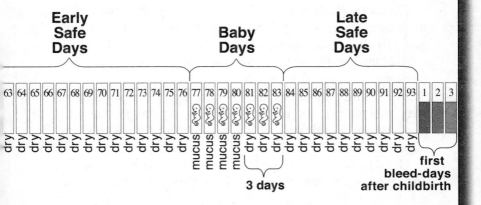

Ruth says, "After the birth of my baby, I felt dry for 76 days. Then on days 77, 78, 79, and 80, I felt wet."

Early Safe Days — Baby Days — Late Safe Days

3 days

first bleed-days after childbirth

The many days from childbirth to mucus are 'Early Safe Days.' During those days Ruth and her husband followed the 'Rules for Early Safe Days.' [page 177]

Elizabeth: My husband and I have enough children. Can we avoid pregnancy by having sex on my bleed-days?

Dear Elizabeth,

No. Sometimes Baby Days begin during bleed-days. (See the 'SHORT' chart on page 178.) So you could get pregnant on bleed-days.

To avoid pregnancy, use Natural Family Planning. This means: Make a new chart for each menstrual-cycle. [pages 169-179]

> Today it's dangerous to have sex on bleed-days.

Dorothy: I'm using Natural Family Planning. My only problem is: Sometimes I feel just a little wet and I think, "Maybe my mucus is starting today... but maybe not... I'm not sure."

In that case what should I do?

Dear Dorothy,

In that case, write on your chart **'mucus?'**. Then avoid sex for three days. During those three days you will see whether or not your mucus has really started.

Example

On day 8 Ruth felt a little wet, and she thought, "Has my mucus started today?" She was unsure. So, on her chart [page 181] she wrote **'mucus?'**.

She let her husband know, and they avoided sex for three days...days 8, 9 and 10.

She found that days 9 and 10 were dry. Then she knew, "My mucus has not yet arrived." So, on day 11 she and her husband continued with sex (obeying the 'Rules' on page 177).

On day 14 she felt wet. Again she wrote **'mucus?'** and she began avoiding sex. This time the wet feeling *continued during days 15 and 16, proving that her mucus had arrived.*

So, she and her husband had no sex on her Baby Days; then they enjoyed sex often during her Late Safe Days.

In this menstrual-cycle Ruth had 'Unsure Days.'

| | | Unsure Days (no sex for 3 days) | | | Baby Days (no sex) | | | Late Safe Days | |

On day 8 I said, "I'm not sure if my mucus has started today." So I wrote **'mucus?'** on my chart, and I avoided sex for three days.

Since days 9 and 10 were dry, I knew my Baby Days had not yet arrived.

On day 14 I felt wet again. I avoided sex. Days 15 and 16 were wet, so I knew my Baby Days had arrived.

Clement: Last year my wife and I agreed, "We will use condoms. We won't use Natural Family Planning. Why? Because we want to have sex on *any* day. We don't want to wait for safe days."

But then we decided to try the Natural way. We discovered, although Natural Family Planning forces us to *wait* some days, *waiting makes sex better*. We enjoy sex more now.

Dear Clement,

Yes, couples who use Natural Family Planning often say, "Sex is even more exciting since we wait for it."

Owen: My brother says, "A woman will not have much interest in sex if she has a baby every year."

Dear Owen,

True. If she has less than two years between pregnancies, she will not have much energy for sex, or for anything. She will always feel weak and tired.

Therefore give your wife a space of two years or more.

Patrick: My wife said, "Our son should reach age 2 before I get pregnant again."

To avoid making her pregnant, I do this: I remove my penis from her vagina before I ejaculate. Then I ejaculate outside, on her thighs.

But now she's pregnant! How???

Dear Patrick,

When a man enters his wife, two things happen.

> **a) Pre-ejaculation.** Soon after he enters, a small drop of <u>clear</u> liquid comes out of his penis. The clear liquid contains a few sperm.

> **b) Ejaculation.** Some minutes later he ejaculates a spoonful of <u>white</u> liquid. The white liquid contains many sperm.

So, Patrick, you cannot prevent pregnancy by removing your penis from her vagina before you ejaculate. Why? Because the <u>clear</u> liquid comes out before you remove your penis. Since the clear liquid has a few sperm, it can make her pregnant.

You need a better method. There are many methods of Family Planning. We think the best one is Natural Family Planning. [pages 169 to 181]

Emmanuel: Family Planning is not new to our people. Our fore-fathers realised that mothers and babies are more healthy if there is a long time between pregnancies. In those days they had various methods of preventing frequent pregnancies. Some of their methods worked — others didn't.

Today our problem is: Many husbands don't use any kind of Family Planning to space their children. As a result, many mothers and children are weak because of short-spaced pregnancies.

We need a good method of Family Planning. A nurse told me, "Don't use the 'Baby Day' method. It doesn't work well."

What method do you recommend?

Dear Emmanuel,

We recommend 'Natural Family Planning.' This is not the same as the 'Baby Day' method the nurse mentioned.

You see, many people write books about methods they call 'Baby Day' or 'Natural.' But some of their 'Baby Day' and 'Natural' methods *don't work*. Women who use those methods still get pregnant.

But 'Natural Family Planning' works. In fact, couples who carefully use this method find that it is 95% effective.

Natural Family Planning is not new. If you talk to people in Asia, Africa and Europe, some of them will tell you,

> "Our custom is, a few weeks before a girl's
> wedding day, her mother (or aunt) tells her,
> 'Listen, I'm going to tell you how to recognize
> your 'wet' days. Why am I telling you?
> So that when you and your husband want a baby,
> you will know the best days for getting pregnant.
> And when you want to avoid pregnancy for 2 or
> more years, you will know how.'"

You are right, Emmanuel, that couples should use Family Planning. There are many methods to choose from. We like 'Natural Family Planning.' Why? It works well, and it is natural. [pages 169-181]

Martha: We love our three sons, but we also want a daughter. What can we do so that our next child will be a *girl?*

Dear Martha,

Each time you have sex, your husband puts many 'girl-producing sperm' and many 'boy-producing sperm' into you. All those sperm *race* to your egg. But only one can enter it.

Martha, you have been pregnant three times, and each time it was a boy-producing sperm that won the race to your egg. But you can help a girl-producing sperm to win the next race. How? Do this:

For each of your cycles make a chart like the one below. [You can learn to make charts by reading pages 169-181.]

Since you want a girl, have sex on your 'first mucus' day. Then, don't have sex for about 8 days (until the end of your Baby Days). Do that in every cycle until you get pregnant. Probably you will have a girl baby.

But if you get another boy, don't worry. God gives you what is best for you. (Jer. 29 [11])

No one should listen to relatives who say, "I wish you had a girl," or "I wish you had a boy,"

Thank God for whatever he gives you.

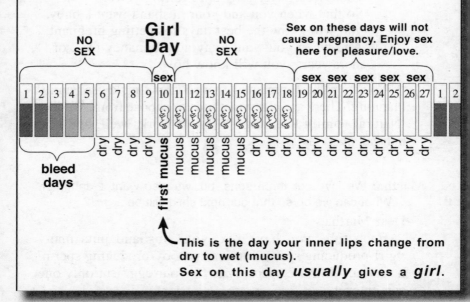

If you want a Girl baby

Read pages 169-181 so you understand 'mucus.' For each of your menstrual-cycles make a chart (similar to this one). In each cycle, have sex on your "first mucus" day. When you get pregnant, probably it will be a girl.

If you want a Boy baby

Read pages 169-181 so you understand 'mucus'. For each of your menstrual-cycles make a chart. In each cycle, have sex on your "mucus decreasing" day.

After six months if you are not yet pregnant, have sex on both your "very wet mucus" day, and your "mucus decreasing" day.

Probably you will get a boy.

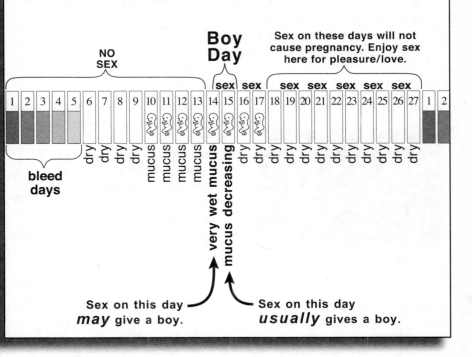

Bernice: My husband is working far away. I'm ashamed to say, yesterday I allowed our son (age 21) to have sex with me.

Now we both feel so guilty; we cannot talk or even face each other.

Dear Bernice,

Tell your son, "This must <u>never</u> happen again."

God says: Don't have sex with your child, sister, brother, half-sister, grandchild, step-mother, son's wife, brother's wife, wife's child, father's sister or brother, mother's sister . . . . (Lev. 18 [6-18], Lev. 20 [11], Deut. 22 [30], 27 [20], 1 Corinth. 5 [1])

Bernice, do this: Pray to Christ. Confess your sins.

Believe that he came from heaven to die for your sins. Accept him as your Lord and Saviour. [page 27] Then help your son and your whole family to do the same.

Pray to Christ. Confess your sins. Believe that he came from heaven to die for your sins. Accept him as your Lord and Saviour. [page 27] Then encourage your son and your whole family to do the same.

Christ will change your lives and your home. And you will live with him in heaven forever. (2 Corinth. 5 $^{17\text{-}21}$)

Peter: Last year my wife was often bitter. Finally I realised: It's my fault! I go everywhere preaching, but at home I'm a selfish husband. So I promised God, "With your help, I will treat my wife with loving kindness."

What an improvement this made in our marriage. And in my preaching!

Caleb: When I die, some of my relatives will try to take all my money and property for themselves, leaving my wife with nothing.

My wife and I agree that there are certain relatives that really need our help. I think the best plan is: When I die, all my money/property should go to my wife. Then she can help those relatives that we agreed to help.

I realise the Bible says: If a husband dies, his wife may re-marry. (1 Cor. 7 $^{39\text{-}40}$, 1 Tim. 5 ^{14})

Dear Caleb,

Yes, a Christian man should have the attitude, "My wife and I are *one*. Therefore, if I die, my money and property should go to my wife." (Gen. 2 ^{24}, Mark 10 $^{7\text{-}8}$)

In the Bible, when Elimelech died, his property remained with Naomi—his wife. Later Naomi sold the property to Boaz—the brother of her late husband. (Ruth 4 $^{2\text{-}4}$) This shows that a man's property goes to his widow. If his brother wants the property, he pays the widow for it.

A Christian wife should have the attitude, "If my husband dies, I will use the money/property to help our children and needy relatives.

> **A husband and wife are <u>one</u>.** (Eph. 5 31) Together they give help to needy relatives. If he dies, their money and property remain with the widow. (Ruth 4 2-4) And she must do all she can to help needy parents and relatives. (1 Tim. 5 8)

I may remain single, but if I ever marry, I will still use that money/property to help our children and needy relatives."

Caleb, the question is: How can you be sure that your wife will get your money and property when you die? Answer: You must write a 'Will' something like this:

I <u>(PRINT YOUR NAME)</u> *of* <u>(YOUR ADDRESS)</u> *do hereby make this my Last Will and Testament. I give and bequeath all of my estate, real, personal and mixed, of every kind and nature, to my wife,* _ _ _ _ (HER NAMES) _ _ _ _

_ _(DATE)_ _ *I hereby set my hand and seal.* _ _ (SIGN YOUR NAME) _ _

We witnesses declare that the above instrument was at the date thereof subscribed by the Testator in our presence and was at the same time declared by him to be his Last Will and Testament, and he is of sound mind/memory.

(A WITNESS SIGNS HERE) _ _ _ _ _ _ _ (HIS/HER ADDRESS) _ _ _ _ _ _ _

(A WITNESS SIGNS HERE) _ _ _ _ _ _ _ (HIS/HER ADDRESS) _ _ _ _ _ _ _

(A WITNESS SIGNS HERE) _ _ _ _ _ _ _ (HIS/HER ADDRESS) _ _ _ _ _ _ _

You may ask a lawyer or bank to help you write a more detailed Will. Some banks give *free* help.

After writing your Will, give it to your wife, and give a copy to a person you trust (e.g. a church-leader).

Stephen: When our baby was sick, we took him to a hospital. Now my uncle tells me, "Don't take your baby to the British doctor. Take him to our own Traditional Healer."

But the 'traditional Healer' says he gets power from the dead. And in the Bible I read that we must not go to people who talk to the dead.

Dear Stephen,

In every country on earth, there are 'Mediums' who claim to get power from the dead. They say, "Come to me if you have problems with illness, money, love, bad luck."

They promise to help your physical needs—they do nothing for your soul.

You are correct: Christians must not go to people who talk to the dead.

> Don't go to a Medium or to anyone who consults the dead, or promises to use power from spirits of the dead to help you, or promises to hurt your enemy. (Deuteronomy 18 [11])

> King Saul died because he was unfaithful to God. He even went to a Medium who talked with the dead. So God put him to death and made David king.
> (1 Chronicles 10 [13-14])

One day while I was in London, I saw in a newspaper a notice from a lady named Anna.

"Anna needs Christ," I said as I picked up my phone.

"Hello, Anna. My name is Bruce. May I pray for you in the loving name of Jesus?"

I feared, "Maybe she will use Satan's power to bewitch me."

Yet I knew, "Satan cannot harm me. Christ is in me." (2 Thes. 3 [3])

> **Anna can help you.**
>
> Do you want success, health, love, a better job, a better marriage . . . ?
> Phone: 817-3119.
> Prophet Anna speaks to relatives who have 'crossed-over.' [died]

After I prayed, she said in a sombre voice, "Jesus told you to call me! I was a church-member, but now I'm doing this sinful job. I know I'll go to hell."

"Come back to Jesus today," I urged. She refused. She enjoyed receiving power from Satan. (Acts 13 [8-10], 16 [16-19])

Do Mediums attend church? Some do. They may say, *"I'm a 'prophet' of God. I talk to the dead, and the dead go to God for me. So my power is really from God."* That's wrong. (Luke 16 [30-31])

The truth is:
Only Jesus can go between us and God.

There is one God, and one person who goes between us and God. That person is the man Jesus. (1 Tim. 2 ^{5}. See also 1 John 2 ^{1})

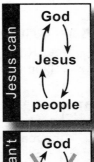

Why talk to the dead on behalf of the living? Go to 'the law and testimony' [Go to 'the Bible'].
(from Isaiah 8 $^{19-20}$)

Don't believe everyone who claims to have the Spirit of God. There are many false prophets.
(1 John 4 ^{1})

Gloria: At age 19 I sinned with a boy. From him I got a sex-disease that damaged my Fallopian tubes. Now I'm married, but I can't get pregnant. Doctors fail to help me. So I paid £400 to a Medium (Traditional Healer), but she has failed too.

Dear Gloria,
Mediums seem to say, *"It doesn't matter if you sin. I have power to remove the trouble that your sins bring to you."* That's not true. (Gal. 6 $^{7-8}$)
Christ says, "Gloria, I died for your sins. Ask me to save you from hell. Trust me to take you to heaven." [pg 27-28]
Maybe God will choose to heal you— or maybe not. If not, he still has an excellent plan for your life, even if you have no children. (Jer. 29 ^{11})

Grace: In some countries today, people continue to circumcise girls. We Christian women declare, "Female Genital Mutilation must be stopped. It is inhuman and a health risk."

Dear Grace,
We agree. In Female Genital Mutilation (FGM) usually the clitoris is damaged or removed. Therefore, FGM is not like male circumcision. When males are circumcised properly, the penis is not damaged (or removed)!
FGM is in-human and a health risk. It must stop.

Ruth: My husband and I are old. Should we stop having sex?

Dear Ruth,

Don't stop. Enjoy sex with each other.

Mercy: After our wedding, my husband grew more and more stubborn. Eventually I asked myself, "Is he like that because he realises I don't love him?"

So I decided to love my husband. When he came home from work discouraged, I was careful to comfort him. I started cooking his favourite meals. In bed I surprised him with playful, sensual love. And when we disagreed on money, I reminded myself to speak respectfully to him.

Now he is changing. He's becoming a really nice husband. I love him. I didn't know marriage could be so romantic.

> *Listen everyone: Decide to love your husband/wife.*
> *See how romance will grow in your marriage!*

Teach this:

Ask one lady in class: "What does a perfect husband do?"

She will reply, "He is faithful to his wife, he loves her, protects her, cares for her...."

Then ask her, "What would you do if you had a perfect husband?"

She will reply, "I would honour him, be faithful to him, love him, and serve him with joy."

Here is good news for you as a Christian.

You have a perfect husband!

Christ is your perfect husband. You are his bride. He

loves you, protects you, cares for you....

What did you say you would do if you had a perfect husband? [Let people reply.]   Now do all of that for Christ.

Paul told a church, "I'm trying to help you to be a *pure bride for Christ*. But it seems you want to be like Eve. You listen to false prophets." (2 Corinth. 11 [2-4])

God told Hosea, "Your wife had sex with other men. They sold her. Now she is a slave. Go, show love to her."

So Hosea paid £330 to buy his wife out of slavery. Then he said to her, "Be faithful. Stay with me. And I will stay with you." (Hosea 3 [1-3])

Dear Christian, you were a slave of Satan. On the day you chose to accept Christ, he used his blood to buy you out of slavery. Now he says, "Be my faithful bride. I will stay with you."

In heaven you will enjoy Christ. (Rev. 19 [6-9])
And here on earth, Christ is your perfect husband.
He loves you, cares for you....
Do this:
Love him. Serve him. Enjoy him.
Teach your children to be his pure bride.
And also:
Husband, love your wife like Christ loves his bride.
Wife, honour your husband like you honour Christ.
(Study Eph. 5 [22-33].)

If you love Christ, read the book:
Arise Boldly with Power. (See page 192.)

Other titles available by Bruce Britten:

For all serious Christians.
Power to do God's work!

Teenagers love this book!
So do parents!

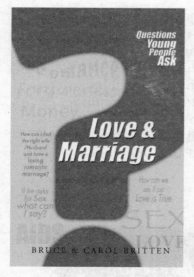

Young people find in this book
the keys to true love.

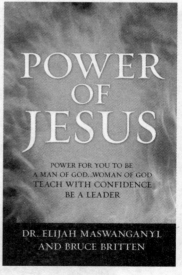

Power for you to be a man
of God...a woman of God.